The Millennial's Guide to the Universe

How to Live the New International Dream

By Natalie Elisha, Esq.

Lois!

always

lets sparkle

together,

XO
Natalie

Table of Contents

Introduction

Why does change win every election?

Why is it always the sexiest term that sets a movement ablaze?

More and more people are realizing that the old systems of the world no longer serve the human condition. The truth is, maybe they never did. The legal, medical, educational and corporate structures that have been in place for the past few centuries are in desperate need of a facelift. The world around us is changing at an alarming rate, and my generation—the Millennial generation—has grown up right in the thick of it. For us, especially, it's easy to see that the old paradigms don't work in a day of rapid change. This book is an attempt to posit a new paradigm.

Of course, I don't claim this short manifesto will solve all the world's problems. That would take a much bigger book, one I'm not qualified to write. However, I hope this purposely short book will start the conversation about the ways in which this much-needed facelift can occur.

So, who is this book for?

- Millennials who are passionate about living an amazing life and shifting the paradigm
- Parents of teenagers that want to ensure the debt epidemic of the Millennial generation is not perpetuated in their children's lifetime
- Teenagers who want the definitive how to on how to structure their life for maximum impact
- People who want a do-over in life
- Anyone with a pulse that wants to once and for all understand how to secure their financial future
- Small businesses and large corporations that want to understand how to encourage a Millennial workforce to expand the foundations they have put into place in their workplaces

Before anything can happen, though, all of the above need to embrace and respect the notion of change.

CHANGE begins on the inside, one person at a time; it starts with changing our own thinking—changing the way *we* approach the world. If only one person is positively affected, I've done my job, but it's my humble wish that many more people are inspired to action, both from my personal story and from the ideas I present in the following pages. I don't want to bore you with filler; I want to give you a short read that can truly incite you to start on your individual journey toward an extraordinary life.

The majority of this book focuses on the education structure because I believe this is the area in the deepest need of surgery. While writing, reading and arithmetic are all extremely important areas on which to concentrate, they only begin to scratch the surface of what a person actually needs to learn to live a fulfilling life.

That said, we learn by stories, so I'll begin this book with the story I know best: mine. It is, I hope, an inspirational one that will set your soul on fire and motivate you to take action in your own life. Throughout my story, I give helpful hints for how you, your kids, grandkids, parents, friends or lovers can explore options to live the life you've always wanted by living what I call the New International Dream.

From there, I will lay out the New Curriculum—a curriculum you won't find in any educational institution, but one which I believe is absolutely vital to living powerfully in this global economy. I'll also lay out the Solution to what I believe could solve four epidemics in our society: the debt epidemic; the recruiting epidemic (i.e., the difficulty of getting new hires); the job epidemic (in which Millennials are relegated to taking second class jobs); and the aging epidemic. When you consider what's possible, it's really a rather simple solution, or at least, I think so.

Finally, I'll present some ideas of how we can incorporate the Millennial generation into the New World Order, into the workforce and into the world. We'll talk about some of the ways the older generations can mentor the younger ones, and we'll discuss how the Millennial approach can bring needed change.

Every important life move I have made has been encapsulated by the following line from the popular Lee Ann Womack song: "When you get the choice to sit it out or dance, I hope you dance." Friends, I am dancing through this small but mighty book. May you dance and live mightily on your own unique and individual stage. May you live mightily in tandem with love.

Thank you for buying and reading this book. I pray that it is as meaningful to your life to read as it was for me to write. We are all mirrors to one another in the world. My hope is that this book shine light on you, and that your life will shine light on all those with whom you come in contact.

Chapter 1: THE NEW INTERNATIONAL DREAM

The American Dream is dead.

No, wait; let me qualify that. The American Dream has expanded.

In my humble opinion, as we shift toward a more global society, our priorities are shifting, as well. As a result, we are moving away from the traditional view of the American Dream and more toward a standard I call the *New International Dream*—an evolved version of the American Dream that is informed by world affairs and the Internet's ability to touch people all over the world.

What Is (or Was) the American Dream?

In our minds, the idea of an American Dream draws its inspiration from our own *Declaration of Independence*, which identifies "life, liberty and the pursuit of happiness" among the "inalienable rights" we all are presumed to have. The actual phrase "American Dream" was first coined in 1931 by James Truslow Adams in his book *Epic of America*, in which he states:

"The American Dream is that dream of a land in which life should be better and richer and fuller for everyone, with opportunity for each according to ability or achievement."

Nowadays, we've come to picture the American Dream almost as a set of status symbols we strive to achieve: The big house (white picket fence optional), the nice car, family vacations, disposable income. It's an ideal that in our world is getting more elusive for many.

Now, what is this New International Dream in comparison? I like to break it down as follows:

- The ability to obtain a great education in subjects that enable you to live a more fulfilled life
- Being fluent in the languages of life (see the New Curriculum)

- Knowing your purpose and living it fully

- The freedom to choose a career that allows you to serve that purpose

- Falling madly in love with your life and the people you allow into it

- The ability to pursue your passion from anywhere in the world

- Not drowning in debt

- Never worrying about money and simply enjoying the time you have on this planet

- Doing good for yourself and others

- Leaving a legacy when you leave (e.g., monetary, spiritual, small, large, whatever you want it to be)

At first glance, perhaps you can see why this ideal has evolved past what we know as the American Dream—and it's not just that we've become a global society. If you stop and think about it, the American Dream has become quite selfish, although it probably wasn't always this way. It's been reduced simply to pursuing our own happiness without much regard for how it affects others. I won't go into details here, but that self-centered mentality actually has a lot to do with the problems we now face in our world, especially in the financial sector. We've grown accustomed to making decisions without considering how others might be affected by those choices.

With the New International Dream, our vision expands in a couple of ways. First of all, *we no longer base our happiness solely on money or financial freedom.* Those elements are still present, but we understand that those things don't necessarily lead to a happy life.

Secondly, *we pursue our own happiness while regarding the well-being of others.* Look at the last two tenets again:

- Doing good for yourself AND OTHERS
- Leaving a legacy when you leave

Can you see how these tenets can lead to a more fulfilled, more powerful life? As a culture—especially, I believe, those of us identified as Millennials—we're growing tired of our own selfishness and our reliance on wealth to pursue happiness. We dream of living within the bigger picture—hence, the New International Dream.

I've titled this book *The Millennial's Guide to the Universe* because I truly believe the collective dream of the Millennial generation (of which I am a part) is being stolen from us by the older educational and financial structures, both of which put us solidly in a debt paradigm as opposed to an abundance paradigm. Too many of us are trying to launch careers while buried in debt, all because of a set of expectations that is no longer relevant. It's time to rethink these structures, along with many others that are holding us back from living a more fulfilled life. (We'll go into more details about this a bit later.)

That said, this book isn't just for Millennials; it's a how-to guide for people of all ages who wish to live their lives more powerfully. It does not matter if you are 9 or 90—you might as well start doing what you want to do now, because the time will pass anyway. In fact, the

"Solution," which we'll present later in the book, relies on people from *all* age groups working collaboratively to bring about positive change.

The idea of the New International Dream doesn't originate with me; this is just a term I'm using to describe paradigm shift that's already happening in our world. The rumblings of this change are already beginning. It's as if everywhere I go, people are talking about the New World Order, the new paradigm that must be pushed through.

Love: The Missing Element

As stated earlier, the New International Dream is an expanded version of the American Dream. It creates context by adding a key element that has long been missing from the old version of the Dream. The missing element is *love*. We love others, and we love ourselves.

You are worthy of love with no judgment. Love is limitless and does not judge. It comes straight from the Creator/Universe/Whatever Energy Force You Believe in, and is the only thing that is real in this world. Every solution on this planet needs love at its base for it to work. When we are loving, we are like the Creator, and in that moment, we create the world we wish.

What would life be like if you believed you had permission to be truly unique, and if you realized you had no chance of failing because you were hand-picked for your own journey? What would life be like if you understood that the future, the present and the past weren't linear and were truly all happening at the same time? And what would life be like if you could live your life in the context of others, gaining wisdom from the prior generation while leaving a legacy for the next?

Don't you want to find out?

The American Dream isn't enough for us anymore. Our world calls us to pursue something more.

The Millennials' Guiding Principles

To make this Dream a reality, we must identify and live by some important guiding principles. Think of it as a new Constitution, a set of rules based on love that forms the foundation for living in this New World Order. Again, these rules are for everyone, not just Millennials, but as the upcoming generation of adults, the Millennials must obviously lead the way. Thus, I refer to these as the **Millennials' Guiding Principles** for living the New International Dream:

1. *Give gratitude to the Creator/GOD/the Universe/Whatever Energy You Believe in, for all that you are.*
2. *Love others, and do not be jealous or in awe of them.* Their success is not a judgment of you; it is their unique journey.

3. *Love yourself unconditionally and find your unique purpose.* Only through self-love can we love others.

4. *Always be awesome and authentic.* It's sexy.

5. *Follow the Platinum Rule: Treat others as they want to be treated.* Ask questions of everyone you meet to find out how they want to be treated.

6. *Have big dreams and goals, and achieve them through rituals and recharging.* Create a "Sabbath" that allows you to cherish how far you've come.

7. *Avoid negative people, debt and hatred like the Plague.*

8. *Understand and respect money so you can bring abundance to your life and protect it once you have it.*

9. *Live as if everything you do is on the world's stage—because it is.*

10. *Honor your word and control your thoughts.* They are all you have. Your word dictates how you show up in the world, and your thoughts control your words.

11. *Question the norm, and always strive for better.* You could be the one whose purpose it is to bring change. In fact, I'm almost certain it's you.

To create a better understanding of these guiding principles and how they can bring change, in the pages ahead we will take a look at some problems with which our governments and societies are currently struggling. We will then review some solutions I believe we must adopt in our world. Along the way, I will include snippets from my personal life, for that is the only story that is authentic to me! My life has given me examples, and I'm sure yours has, too. Please feel free to make these guiding principles your own and draw from your own stories as you read this book. Always trust your story the most, and remember that you can do anything. Also, I welcome you to send your stories to me so that when I re-publish this book in future editions, I can include your amazing story in the right section.

Now for a bit more of my personal story. Please enjoy reading the inner light of my soul. It might not be a perfect piece of literature, but it certainly is the best I know.

Chapter 2: START WITH WHY

My life took an unexpected turn one summer day—specifically, on August 20, 2004. I began the day as a teenager, but by the time I awoke the next day, I had transformed into an attorney, author, speaker and light bearer for the world. (I simply had not manifested those things yet.)

It was a Friday, early evening. The sun was shining. I was a tanned fifteen-year-old wearing a halter top and flip flops, my curly, dirty blonde hair bouncing around my shoulders. I was walking home—the hot and humid two-mile walk between my job as an ices server and my childhood home—to make it for our weekly Shabbat dinner. I was proud. I had just received my pay, a whopping $120 dollars for two weeks of work. I was proud of my paycheck, proud that I didn't have to ask my parents for money. Even then, I was an independent woman who wanted never to rely on anyone, not even my parents, for help.

It was an hour before sundown. I began crossing a street…

That street was the dividing line between who I was and who I was meant to be.

Before I made it across, I was hit full-force by a car traveling at about 60 miles per hour. The driver was a guy who was drag racing his car from light to light; he allegedly never saw me. In that moment, I was transformed from a vibrant teenager to a bloodied, broken child who could no longer could walk, feed or dress herself.

Remarkably, I survived. The hospital staff said they had never seen someone survive such a horrific accident. When I woke up, my first image was that of my mother, hovering above me, crying.

I remember wondering: *Was I dead and in heaven?* If this was heaven, why was my Mom here, and why was she crying? Where was I?

My mother told me that my father was crying too. That really broke me because the only other time I had seen my father cry was at my baby brother Gabriel's funeral. What had happened to me that caused a man I viewed as unbreakable to be weeping in the corner?

The next few days were a blur for me, going in and out of surgeries, zonked out on morphine and still in a state of complete despair and disbelief at what had happened. As I eventually came back to a state of consciousness, my mother made me promise this would be the only time in my life that I would be high. I promised.

It was a sea of faces, family, friends, lawyers who came to visit me as I laid helpless in that hospital bed. I was dressed in a hospital gown, which is one step above pure nakedness, watching this stream of people look at me with sorrow in their eyes. Their sorrow was really about feeling sorry for me: *This poor girl, her poor family, how could this happen, well, thank God it didn't happen to my family.* These were the things their eyes said to me.

I wish I could tell you I was superwoman, at least on the inside. I wish I could tell you that I stayed strong and positive. But I didn't. The truth is, I felt as broken on the inside as I was on the outside. I struggled with the questions. Well, actually, it was one question, phrased in many different ways: **Why?**

Why had this happened to me?

Why God had chosen to do this to me? How could an all-loving God have forced me into a handicap that I knew would affect me for my entire life?

And **why**, if I was going to be in an accident like this, had he chosen for me to survive it? Didn't he know the pain it was causing me and my family to see me in this position?

Why?

I was at a crossroads.

I was either going to look at this circumstance as my greatest blessing or my greatest curse. After all, aren't they two sides of the same coin?

I had been spared from death. What would I do with the rest of my life?

One way or the other, what had happened to me would shape my life forever. It was now part of my story, inextricably linked to who I was, and who I was going to be. There was no denying its impact. As to *how* it would affect my story—that was really up to me.

I could see myself either as a victim or as a miracle. With the metal rods, plates and pins they placed in me to hold me together, I was either a patched-up shell of a human, or I was bionic, fantastic. I could either give up and fall into depression, or I could decide right then and there to change the world, bringing light and angel wings to all of those on my path.

It was one or the other, no middle ground. As Yogi Berra famously said, "When there is a fork in the road, take it."

You can guess what I chose. I chose the light and the angel wings. I decided to allow this event to be a blessing and not a curse. That day, I started walking, or rather *wheeling* (in my wheelchair), on my new path.

It took some time, but eventually I made a full recovery. I still have four pieces of metal inside me, but I'm no longer in a wheelchair or braces. Spiritually and emotionally, the impact continues—I'll never be the same. But because I chose to see this event as a miracle—because I allowed it to empower me rather than victimize me—my life changed exponentially for the better. Since that moment, and that *decision*, I've been able to do more than I probably ever would had I not crossed that street. Here are just a few of the headlines of what has happened since that day:

- I finished high school with high honors and multiple awards as a student of one of the most prestigious high schools in the country, Townsend Harris High School (yes, I am a nerd forever and always).
- I went to Binghamton University, where I made my lifelong friendships and excelled, both academically and socially. I earned a bachelor's degree in two years with a *magna cum laude* designation, and went on to get full scholarship offers at multiple law schools.
- I attended St. John's University School of Law, where I won awards regionally for negotiation and mediation techniques, became a teaching assistant for Negotiation, graduating with honors at 23 years old, after being offered a full scholarship...DEBT FREE!

- By age 23 years old, I became one of the youngest people in the country admitted to the practice of law. I had a great job, debt free, first working in-house for a real estate development company, then at a law firm.

- At age 24, I started my own law firm, turning it into a 7-figure firm within two years.

- At age 27, I was ranked as a Rising Star-Super Lawyer in New York in the fields of Estate Planning and Probate and took a week sabbatical to Hawaii to write this book; and

- Now, at the ripe old age of 28, I purchased a condo in Miami so that I could expand my law practice and tour the world teaching about my New Curriculum to really help bring about change in this world.

I don't list these achievements in order to brag, but simply to share what is possible. As we move through this book, I'll show you how accomplished all this, and how you can accomplish the same things, if you wish—or your own version of them. For now, the point I want to make is that you don't have to go through a horrific accident like I experienced—because the truth is, the accident itself wasn't the turning point in my life. Rather, it was the inevitable question that followed:

Why?

For me, the *why* went from "*Why* did this happen to me?" to "*Why* am I still here?"

Which, if you think about it, actually translates to, "*Why* am I alive? What is my purpose?"

And isn't that the question we all carry in our hearts? The question we all need to answer?

One of my favorite authors of all time, Simon Sinek, in his world-renowned book *Start with Why*, theorizes that a company that starts with *why* is most able to differentiate themselves in the marketplace—to understand fully their value proposition to their customers and to themselves. In other words, the passion for *why* you do what you do attracts the right customers because you become the right company. I have so resonated with Simon Sinek's message that I have applied his philosophy not only to my business, but also to my very life. Perhaps it's because of my own moment of truth—the moment that forced me to consider *why* I was on the planet, and what I was going to do about it. The fact that I had survived something that by all accounts should have killed me brought my own *why* to the center of my thoughts. It just so happened that the time spent in that hospital bed gave me time to come to grips with my decision.

So here's my own personal *why*:

I am on this planet to bring limitless love, understanding and purpose to the people I touch in my personal and professional life so that I may inspire, educate and elevate them to live their dream.

My desire to be this light for others so permeates everything that I do that it doesn't matter which role I am playing in my life. Whether I am a daughter, sister, leader, attorney, friend, lover, speaker, coach or professor—my *why* is always consistent.

Reader, I hope you understand that the car that hit me represents every man and woman's obstacle—that thing that tries to stop each of us. What is it for you? Is it the bully from elementary school, the divorced parents, the failed relationships, the lie that you have been told that you are not good enough, the grades you used to get, the lack of love that have been your reality? For me, it was a drag- racing car, and it had every opportunity to squeeze out my positive outlook, take from me my passion for living and ruin my life. Or, as I decided, it was a reminder that life is fleeting. Life is there for the living, and we cannot wait even one moment to live our dream. I resolved in that moment never to waste time living someone else's dream. After all, I had just received my angel wings, and I was now a miracle worker. I could do anything. And so, I did. And more importantly, so can you.

But it starts with *why*. It starts with your story, and the obstacles in it, which ultimately leads you to your purpose.

Your own story is PERFECT for you. My story could not have been, "Natalie got hit by a car and then built a 7-figure law firm by 26 and now is writing this book to encourage, empower and inspire the young people today that they can do anything in this world" unless that story was MEANT for me. This is my *why*. The Creator, the Almighty, whatever you want to call the spiritual energy that is out there, destined me to walk this path and have these experiences so I can speak and write about them in the hope that it awakens even one person who is overwhelmed, sad, discouraged, depressed or uncertain of themselves and their path.

So regardless of what you've been through, and what you might feel is currently trying to stop you—let it lead you to your why. Find your truth.

And here's a tip: *To live your authentic truth, do not do what everyone else is doing.* That is ordinary, and it will not lead to extraordinary results. In fact, as you'll see in the pages ahead, this book aims to address what I call the *anti-herd*—those who purposely are NOT walking the path others have walked. When people talk about being "outside the box," I laugh because those people are repeating some canned phrase that shows they certainly are in the box. (Tip Number Two: *There is no box!*)

My story isn't quite over. Let me share a bit more about how I stopped letting fear run my life, and how I could stop being paralyzed as I walked up the staircase…that staircase of life many on which so many of us are immobilized.

Chapter 3: FIFTEEN LITTLE STEPS

When I first came home from the Intensive Care Unit, after my accident I was in a wheelchair. My parents put me in the basement area with the bed that the hospital had shipped so they could take care of me.

One day, a few days before 10th grade was supposed to start, we had a follow up appointment with my orthopedic surgeon, a man whom I believe truly was an angel and saved my life. My dad wasn't home the day of my appointment, and my mom certainly couldn't lift me up the 15 steps that separated the basement from the exit of my house. So it was up to me to climb them.

Fifteen steps separated me from the rest of the world.

FIFTEEN LITTLE STEPS.

The ascent up those fifteen stairs took almost twenty minutes, each of which felt like its own lifetime. I cried hysterically the entire way. My mother's heart was breaking as she looked on helplessly, unable to do anything for her daughter but stay by my side as I struggled up one grueling step at a time.

Fifteen steps. One step at a time.

Can you imagine what it would be like to be 15 years old, profoundly injured, barely able to walk, looking up a flight of steps which you see as insurmountable on your own? Can you imagine that all you had to do to reclaim your life, to rejoin all of the other beautiful people in the world, was to get yourself up those FIFTEEN LITTLE STEPS? How does one manage it?

One step at a time.

For the second time in my life, I had the opportunity to learn how to walk, how to climb steps. I couldn't climb fifteen steps. But I could climb one.

And then I could climb another.

And another.

Slowly but surely, I was remembering what it is to be able to walk. If I hadn't understood what it is to be a human and be alive before that moment, I understood it completely and perfectly in those twenty minutes, slowly making my ascent to reclaim the rest of my life.

For me, those fifteen little steps represented much more than learning how to climb stairs again. This was the obstacle standing between me and my purpose. If I could get out of the basement by myself, I could get to the other places I needed to go. I could get out and begin living my purpose. But I had to climb those steps, one by one. There was no other way.

We each have a staircase to climb—a set of steps that represents our path to leading a successful life. Taken together, the steps might seem insurmountable. Fear and intimidation may overwhelm us, but if we want to reach our purpose, we must climb. The only alternative is to stay in the basement.

But here's the good news: You don't have to take all fifteen steps at once. In fact, you can't. No one can take fifteen steps at once.

But you can take one at a time.

Learning to Walk

For us to understand success truly, we must go back to our past, back to the time where we were still crawling, unable to move much because we were undeveloped. Our parents had legs that worked. We had them too, but they were of unknown power to us.

Can you remember the time before you could walk? If your memory doesn't go that far back into your childhood, just try and imagine it. One day, when you were maybe 10-12 months old, you decided to explore. You decided that you were going to take that first step. You were going to do it! You started and stopped and started and fell, but every time you got back up.

Can you imagine the achievement, the sense of power and joy that the one-year-old you must have been feeling? *I can walk, I can run, I can move. I am POWERFUL. I am LOVE. I am CAPABLE. If I can accomplish this, I can accomplish ANYTHING and EVERYTHING.*

What happened to us since that time? What have we forgotten? Once we learn how to walk, we completely take it for granted. We no longer view it as a prize or achievement. Inexplicably, we no longer appreciate our magnificence. We are the only animals in the animal kingdom who walk exclusively on two legs. Why do we not give gratitude for this miracle until the time it's taken away from us, and we have to re-learn it?

It was taken away from me.

At fifteen years old, I was unable to walk, shower or feed myself. My ability to walk was stripped from me, not just because of my accident, but because when you don't do something every day, your body literally forgets how to do it.

Let me say that again…

When you stop doing something you do regularly, your body forgets how to do it.

To borrow an overused phrase: If you don't use it, you lose it.

Consider for a moment the implications of this. I forgot how to walk, and I had to learn again. What else can we forget when we don't put it into practice?

LOVE?

COURAGE?

PASSION?

DRIVE?

EXCELLENCE?

ACHIEVEMENT?

AWESOMENESS?

What if we lived every single day like it was the first and last one would ever experience? Imagine it: With this fresh set of eyes and with this amount of gratitude for being alive, wouldn't we cherish our ability to walk and talk and eat and kiss and love and change and create? How much better would life be?

So…What's your staircase? What stands in your way? What do you feel imprisons you?

Is it an injury, like mine was? Or something less obvious? Is it that you don't have the right education? The right physique or figure? Is it that you don't have a lot of money? Is it that you aren't popular?

What are the FIFTEEN LITTLE STEPS that separate you from who you are and who you want to be? Let's figure that out and obliterate those steps. Run, skip, jump, crawl or climb. Do whatever you must do to get past your barriers and start living your amazing life.

You Are Enough

Look at that obstacle for a moment. Put it into perspective. It's remarkable how many excuses we make for why we can't do something, or why aren't enough. Does a piece of paper, a diploma, a dollar, a card, a gift, a "like" on Facebook, makes any ounce of difference to who you truly are right now?

NO.

Those things might give you some credential, some feeling within yourself that you are enough. But what if I told you that you already were enough? That you were already 100% perfect? That the one-year-old you, that infant, knew that every ounce of power you needed was inside of you, and all you needed to do to start walking was stop being afraid of falling?

If we could transport ourselves back to that time and think about our FIFTEEN LITTLE STEPS that stand between us and everything we could do to shift our lives, the lives of our family and the course of world history, wouldn't we tackle those steps with power, light and love every single day?

OF COURSE WE WOULD.

To get up the FIFTEEN LITTLE STEPS, we need an understanding of who we are and what our purpose is. We need to give ourselves permission to be successful in a different way than the "prescription" or "formula" that we were taught.

But there's more. Once we climb those steps, we must come together in community to live a different way. This is where the New Curriculum and the Solution will come in, as we'll discuss later. Our power is in the collective WE. No man or woman is an island.

My story is not one that you must follow; my story is mine. I simply want to give you options and encouragement that the *ONE* path we have all been told about where success lies— that is, College, Grad School, One House, Same Job Until We Retire, Social Security and

Pension Plans taking care of us in the future—that path is *NOT* the only way (in fact, it may no longer even be a reality). I want to suggest a different route to get to a successful life—if you will, a walk up a staircase toward your own success. By *successful*, I mean a life that allows you to live the New International Dream, as we defined earlier. This is a roadmap to the anti-herd, anti-box culture that I foresee will be the only way to "make-it" in the coming years.

In my own life, I figured out a way to climb my ladder of success in a non-traditional way. What if we could accomplish the goals of being educated and well employed and happy in a way that is different than the way that we think it is today? Shouldn't we at least try to do it better?

What if those FIFTEEN LITTLE STEPS represent our opportunity to learn how to walk all over again?

What if we realized exactly what our purpose was and what steps we had to take to fulfill it? What if we knew exactly the right person to meet to make the next step possible? What if it were guaranteed?

IT IS.

But in order to reach that purpose, we must rid ourselves of the modern-day incarceration the generations-old prescription for "living a good life" that has been passed down for generations—the "American Dream," if you will. This prescription is flawed, and while it may have worked in prior years, it no longer works today. We are told to fail fast and fail often. Our current education, legal and medical systems have allowed us to fail slowly, fail often and die miserably.

Let's change that. Let's live a different dream.

But first, we each have some steps to climb.

Whatever that means to you, don't let fear keep you in the basement. I'm not saying it will be easy, but if all that stands between you and your destiny are FIFTEEN LITTLE STEPS, isn't it worth the climb?

Besides: It's not fifteen all at once. It's just one at a time.

Chapter 4: THE MODERN-DAY INCARCERATION

It was January 2017. I was sitting in a conference at the Manhattan Chamber of Commerce right next to the keynote speaker, Congressman Hakeem Jeffries. Hakeem is a very accomplished Congressman. He was talking a lot about incarceration, the new President and some other political points. I raised my hand and got to ask the last question of the conference.

"Hakeem, what about the modern-day incarceration?" I asked him. "What about the student loan and debt crisis that is occurring?" I told him that as an alumni speaker and coach at Binghamton University and St. John's University School of Law, often my students would speak to me about the fears that they had about their debt and whether they would ever be able to repay it.

He answered quite charismatically that he was the first congressman to come from Binghamton, which forged an immediate connection between us. He also said that he was very aware of this problem and that the government was doing what they thought they could to alleviate it.

Bernie Sanders, and the revolution of realization he started, have already begun to change things for the better. In fact, here in New York, a law was just passed that will make public college free statewide for many young people. It's a great step forward, but let me explain to you why the debt epidemic is the single biggest incarceration scheme that has ever come to this planet.

First, let's consult the dictionary.

INCARCERATION:
incarceration
in_kärs__r_SH(_)n/
noun
the state of being confined in prison; imprisonment.

When we usually think of this word, we think of something that happens to a criminal after he or she has committed a crime like rape, murder, theft, etc., and now has been brought to justice. These incarcerated individuals are now being housed and fed by the government, sometimes for decades, all on the taxpayer's dime.

Now, let's turn to the modern-day college graduate. Let me explain how these law-abiding citizens, these people who want to make their lives better, who want to live the so-called American Dream, are really the people being incarcerated (especially if they lack vision in what it is they want out of their college education).

Our American Dream has transformed into a reality where an eighteen-year-old is expected to start a journey lasting between four (Bachelor's Degree) and twelve years (Plastic Surgeon), all while not making any money and instead paying hundreds of thousands of dollars to get this education in order to "live a better life." Six months after leaving school, this young man or woman has to start paying back the debt, regardless of whether the job he/she obtains actually provides enough income to do so. Given the exorbitant costs of education these days, it could take decades before the loan is repaid.

Why is it that tuition costs have gone up more than one-thousand percent in the past few decades? Why is it that no other sector besides college has come close to that percentage increase? It's simple for me to understand: College is sold to us as a necessary prerequisite to be successful. This has created an unlimited demand, and prices have skyrocketed as a result. It's simple supply and demand economics.

"Getting an Education" has become the baseline of the alleged success everyone is looking for. However, for many students who go in to college without a clear path, college has actually become a one-way path to financial upheaval for many. The worst part is that the government will give you money freely in the form of student loans, and you can take as much debt as you need for this college education. You can never get rid of this debt, not even in bankruptcy, until it is repaid. This doesn't affect the super wealthy or the super poor—it mostly affects the great middle class which is disappearing. Those who used to reside in this category are just becoming imprisoned by college debt, and therefore, with few exceptions, never able to make the leap to being rich.

As middle-class students become increasingly burdened by growing debt, they cannot figure out how to live the rest of their dreams and truly supercharge their lives. They must pay back this debt, or else. Over the next 30-40 years, they are destined to a life where they are paying back their debt in drips and drabs, unable to do much else. Talk about a guarantee for the government and the needs of corporations to keep workers in seats so those corporations can continue to drive profits.

Can you imagine being a prisoner to this kind of life for 40 years, all because you wanted to get an education and better your life? Imagine what wings you would grow immediately if you didn't have those concerns.

Why has this ridiculous notion of applying for all this debt been accepted in our society? Do you realize that if you went into any bank for any other kind of loan, they would never approve that loan based on your qualifications? The banks want to make sure they will be repaid with interest, and the only reason they give these kinds of loans to students is that the government guarantees them. But what happens when the middle-class student reneges on this promise? What happens when she can't find a job and can't pay her debt—something which happens more frequently these days than ever before? The colleges who charged the high tuition—offer no "money-back guarantees," and of course they aren't willing to go into their own deep endowments in order to help their students. As a result, millions of promising young people are being swallowed alive by their debt.

Why are so few people running debt assumptions before they take on hundreds of thousands of dollars in student debt? Why is no one simply going online and Google what their loan repayment will look like over the course of their lives? Why aren't parents teaching their children about what this kind of debt really means?

Can you see how quickly the process spirals? You pay in excess of $200,000 for a degree from private college, which is basically an expensive pre-requisite for many jobs. However, even with the degree, many corporations still won't give you a decent-paying job because you don't have "experience." You're told the answer is *more* education, so you continue making your mistake by taking on more debt for graduate studies. By the time you finish, the jobs you want are no longer available because the market is too saturated, so you are still going to have to take a lower paying job to start paying back your debt. Welcome to prison.

This cannot be our prized American Dream. Yet, remarkably, it's the dream we're being sold. What has happened to the place where people come to dream, to open their minds, to embrace love, to build a future that their ancestors could never reach?

So now let's ask a different question, and maybe it will help us change our thinking: Why do you suppose so many of the richest people in the world are business owners?

Do you see it? The world's richest people aren't college-graduate employees. They are the *employers*. They aren't the ones looking to be hired—they're the ones doing the hiring.

And here's the thing: You don't necessarily *need* a degree to be a business owner. Of course, if you want to own a law firm, medical practice or accounting firm, you'll need that particular credential, but for the most part, the super-successful people, the multi-millionaires and billionaires, are not lawyers, doctors or accountants. (Or more accurately, they are not practicing as such.) They *might* have the formal education, but in many cases their education is irrelevant.

You see, being an employee—and in many cases, being on staff at a law firm or at a hospital—these jobs place you in the service businesses. That's not where the real money is. The service business model by nature ties your dollars to time. The *real* money is in the scalability and replicability of your business.

That is a successful business person—the one who scales his business. Examples include Steve Jobs, Mark Zuckerberg, Elon Musk. Do these people have every client calling them? Do these people have to be the sales person for their product each and every day? Of course not. It would never happen. Why? They learned how to scale their business, to grow it to the point of delegating that work to others. They then get to reap the rewards.

That sounds more like the American Dream to me—or by our own definition, the *New International Dream*—than any part of the path we're collectively being told to follow.

So why is it that we are led to believe that taking out hundreds of thousands in debt (which becomes millions by the time we pay it back), is the American Dream? Why have we allowed this fraud? Why haven't we stopped and said we are better than this?

I have news for you…We ARE better than this. We don't have to live this life.

Now, let me make one thing abundantly clear. A college education **IS** an amazing thing. It stretches your mind, allows you to build lifelong friendships and gives you a solid foundation for your life. However, haphazardly choosing a college and then a major without doing the cost benefit analysis, and even more primitively, without understanding what the job actually requires from you, is absolutely foolish.

I am **NOT** suggesting that people should not go to college. If you or your child has a clear path in mind and has done internships and understands what needs to be done to get to where they want to be, by all means get the best education possible. This message is not for those students who **KNOW** they will do one thing or another, no matter what. This message is for those children and their parents who just don't know. There isn't a problem with not knowing. Go…**EXPLORE, ADVENTURE!**

Don't, though, go spending $60,000 a year to party and allow yourself not to figure it out. A year or so to find yourself and do some travel is fine and in the long run, will save the student thousands of dollars in debt obligations. The theory that at 18 years old, a person **MUST** know what they want, is absolutely absurd. Take **TIME** to figure this out and do not take on debt during the figuring out period.

Alvin Toffler, in his world-renowned book *The Third Wave*, speaks about the three waves of society at large, which he defines as the Agricultural, Industrial and Information Ages, respectively. As of the writing of this book, we are exiting the Second Wave (Industrial) and entering the Third Wave (Information). The arrival of the Information Age is clear; it has been realized as a result of the Internet, innovation and "disruption" of multiple industries. The progress of the Third Wave and the capacities now available to us are truly promising and enlightening.

The problem is that the Second Wave—the Industrial Age upon which our education systems are based—is holding on for dear life.

Toffler presents proof in his book that our current education system is based squarely in the paradigms of the Industrial Age. The overt educational curriculum is based on reading, writing and arithmetic, but it really was designed to get students to sit down, shut up and become good factory workers. This had to be the case so they could work on the assembly line without questioning authority. In our current emerging Information Age, the same exact curriculum is at the forefront and perhaps even worse (Common Core—ever heard of it?). Is it any wonder why some of the most successful people in the Information Age have bypassed this system almost entirely?

In the true Industrial Age, college wasn't all that expensive, largely because many people didn't go to college. It was truly just a handpicked group of stellar students whose families did not have to worry about their child/spouse making money for survival. These people did very well and ended up running the companies which are the modern-day successes. Many of the smartest among these college students continued on to law and medical school in order to extend the academic and societal gifts they enjoyed.

And then, like any good money-making secret, people caught on! If *everyone* went to college, everyone would be able to have these opportunities! In theory, it was a wonderful idea. In time, though, the colleges noticed the influx of applicants and rearranged their tuition numbers accordingly. Those high-paying jobs in the more honorable professions became scarcer as the market became oversaturated—and yet, the colleges kept pushing their agenda on unsuspecting students, holding out the elusive carrot of a high-paying job because the government was underwriting their debt. And that basically catches us up to where we are in modern-day society.

As demand increased, College and Graduate School became the newest hits. Higher education is still the biggest hit—the success drug, the "prescription." Supposedly, I can take this prescription and POOF!—just like that, my life is set, and I will be successful. Some people spend hundreds of thousands of dollars on tutors to get their kids into the right college, and then they continue to pay hundreds of thousands of dollars for that college while the college gives a zero-money back guarantee. Meanwhile, many college graduates today are lucky if they can get a job that pays more than minimum wage.

And to add insult to injury—if you cannot find gainful employment, the college that once embraced you and your student loans with open arms now tells you it is *your* fault you can't get a high paying job. Meanwhile, as an alum of that school, you'll now start getting the bimonthly calls for donations to their generous endowments, which they *won't* be using to help other students go to school. In most cases, endowments go to nothing but new facilities and to fund professors' "research."

Research is a necessary tool, but is it really necessary on the college campus? Or could it be done more effectively at a separate institution with a budget that is not being underwritten by Millennial debt? But I digress.

Many mortgage bankers say that buying a house is the biggest investment their customers will ever make. While that might have been true 20 years ago, it is now clearly false. Many Millennials are so busy paying back their student loan debt that they will never even make it to buying a house. Today, your education will be your biggest investment, especially if you attend a private institution or a state college in a state where you are not a resident. And even if you do eventually get a mortgage, chances are that student loan will remain your biggest investment for the rest of your life.

When you buy a house, you have a physical structure which allows you to be safe from the elements and other people—a place where you can raise a family, make memories and spread love. What does your expensive college education give you?

Actually, a modern-day college education offers three things: an **educational foundation**, **experience** and **access**. Let me further flesh these out:

- An **educational foundation** is the well rounded degree that a Bachelor's degree represents. It is the symbol to show employers (and the world) that you had the discipline to achieve the diploma.
- **Experience** refers to the so-called "college experience" (i.e., sex, drinking, drugs, Greek life, athletics, growing up, studying abroad); and
- **Access** refers to having access to job opportunities. Although this trend is rapidly diminishing, the college degree gives you a measure of qualification so you can apply for most jobs that pay slightly higher than minimum wage.

And in bullet point three (access) lies the real problem: students get *access* to jobs but not a guarantee—and even if they get hired, the job may not pay enough to cover the debt. The colleges are not the only ones to blame. Corporations have also bought in to the notion that a college degree makes a person better situated to perform job tasks well. More and more research is coming out to show that there is actually no correlation. Prestigious companies are now looking towards "soft skills" and the ability to code as more important than a degree. Again, this is not to say that College is a bad thing. It is to say that not everyone needs a college degree in order to be "successful".

We mentioned supply and demand economics earlier. There is a limited supply of schools because for an institution to become accredited as a university, that institution has to jump through certain hoops. Most of these institutions cannot afford to pay millions of dollars in legal fees to get approved as university by the government, so this keeps the *supply* of universities limited. There may be a few hundred such schools around the country. People all around the country are vying for those seats, which means the *demand* is virtually unlimited.

When supply is limited and demand is outrageous, it creates scarcity, so naturally the prices go up. Colleges have been run well enough to understand this epidemic, and they capitalize on this. Big time.

What Are the Alternatives?

Now, this is probably not earth shattering news; we all collectively agree and understand that college is too expensive...but what can we do instead? The good news is, there are several alternatives, and we'll go into more details when we get to The New Curriculum and The Solution. For now, here are some ways we Millennials can circumvent this modern-day incarceration:

1. We can graduate school earlier and thereby significantly lessen our debt obligations.
2. We can get full scholarships to college.
3. We can skip traditional education altogether.
4. We can work for small businesses whose hiring may not be as stringent.
5. We can start our own businesses.
6. We can convince the corporations to change their hiring requirements, basing them on qualifications and merit rather than on holding a college degree, thereby giving access to more potential hires. In this way, we could eradicate the student loan epidemic and solve the recruiting hassles as well as make strides in the aging epidemic. (This is my favorite option, and I'll detail it a bit more in The Solution.)

To see how some of these alternatives can play out, let me offer some advice and "system hacks" for those pursuing formal education, based on some of my own experiences. If you happen to be an adult who already has a job or career, this information may not directly apply to you, but it could be helpful for starting a conversation with your children about their future, or even if you're thinking to go back to school yourself.

THE TWO-YEAR BACHELOR DEGREE

When people find out I graduated college in two years with a double major, I usually get one of these responses from them:

- *"Wow, you must be a genius or prodigy!"* (I wish; usually I follow this one up with a joke about how my hair is fake-blonde.)
- *"You graduated with a bachelor's degree in two years?"* (YES.)
- *"You must have never gone out."* (False; I was probably one of the biggest party girls in Binghamton and went out a minimum of five nights a week. I also was the President of my dorm, pledged a sorority and eventually served as its social and philanthropy chairs, and was extremely involved in the Jewish scene on campus).
- *"How?"* (Ready to take notes?)

I would love to tell you that I graduated in two years because I am a genius, but I am not. (Besides, my father, who ensured that I completely understood what the word "humble" meant, would kill me if I ever professed to be one.) Rather, as you're about to see, everything I've achieved has come by figuring out the systems and using them to my benefit. So now that we have dispelled the idea that I am in some way special, I am here to show you how YOU can do the same thing!

A quick note before we move on: The material covered in this chapter and the next will obviously be of the most benefit to young people currently pursuing their education. However, if you're an adult who already has a job or career, this information may be helpful for starting a conversation with your children about their future, or even if you're thinking to go back to school yourself.

Understanding the College System

The college curriculum is a system that mandates the meeting of certain requirements to finish with a bachelor's degree. What are some of these requirements?

1. Approximately 126 credits (varies slightly depending on the school);
2. General education requirements;
3. Required courses to complete your major; and
4. Residency requirements (i.e., the number of classes you actually have to take on campus to qualify for a degree from that school).

Some schools have additional requirements, but for the most part, they basically fall into one of the above referenced categories.

Now, to get through college quickly, it helps to have one of two goals in mind. You should either:

- Have a clear understanding of the career you want; or

- Have no idea, but have an immense desire to finish quickly to save money, and then figure out your career afterward (if this is you, you may want to consider doing some soul searching before jumping in to a college education that may not fully suit your wishes)

Either way, having a clear objective will make it a million times easier to get there. No matter how fancy the GPS app is on your phone, it cannot correctly guide you if you don't input an address, a landmark or at least an intersection. By the same token, you'll have a more difficult time finding your way to an early graduation without an established destination in mind.

But why do it?

Now that we know it is possible, why would anyone choose to graduate college so early? Perhaps for any of the following reasons:

1. You want to get on with your life and start traveling the world or working in your family business; or
2. You want to take on as little debt as possible; or
3. You want to continue partying with your sports team/ fraternity/sorority without having to worry about classes anymore; or
4. You want to take the money that otherwise would have been used for years 3 and 4, buy a house with it and rent the rooms to your friends to pay your mortgage (Presto! Your very first business venture!); or

5. Your startup has the potential of being bought by Facebook but you still want a bachelor's degree "just because"; or

6. You have to take care of a sick parent or sibling; or

7. You want to get married and start a family; or

8. You just want to.

Any of these are great reasons to graduate early, you may have a reason or two of your own, but if not, feel free to borrow these for your own use.

So how do you move from understanding that a 2-year bachelor's is possible, to attaining it?

Simple: You PLAN.

What did you guys think I would say? It's a lot of hard work. This isn't a fantasy novel. It's real life. Planning and hard work will get you a long way.

The Planning Process

Once you're clear in your mind about your intentions and why you want to graduate early, here's what you should do to plan for it.

High School

If you want to graduate college early, the planning process should really start in high school for best results. The most important things to figure out for yourself in high school are:

- What are you naturally good at that you could see yourself enjoying if you made a career out of it?
- What is your "dream job?"

If you don't know the answers to these two questions yet, I smell internships in your future. I also recommend the Impact Circles as an amazing place to get your feet wet with understanding what kind of jobs are available in the world! (More on this later in "The Solution.")

Once you have an idea about what you want to do in life, start researching colleges that offer programs geared around those interests. Consider all factors, not just academics. For example, will you be living with or near your parents? Do you have the ability to stay in a dorm? Do you have a preference as to climate or area of the country?

Another factor to consider is whether the college allows for the transfer of College Now Credits and/or Advanced Placement Courses. If it does, take plenty of these courses in high school, but if you have your heart set on a school that does not count those classes for credit, don't waste your effort. The reverse is also true: If you already have a ton of AP credits, look into colleges that affirmatively take them. In this way, you should be able to enter college with a minimum of 12 and a maximum of 30 credits already completed. By following this strategy, I walked into college with 27 credits completed. That's one year down!

College

You have sent out your college applications, and you have received one or more acceptance letters. Congratulations! What's next?

- *Choose the college that gives you a great nexus of the things you are looking for.* Factors to consider are good location, great job prospects, and whether the college gives credit for your high school Advanced Placement and College Now courses, as we discussed.
- *Decide on your major.* Figure out which of the AP classes you have already taken can go towards that major, and any and all other requirements the school might have.
- *Do not take any classes that do not perfectly align with your intention to graduate early.* Each class should fulfill at least 2 of your degree requirements; the more, the better. For instance, I would take classes at college that counted towards 4 separate requirements. (Yes, this means you have to go through the course catalog a few times, but isn't it worth saving two years of your life and thousands of dollars?)
- *Go into orientation with a schedule planned, a backup plan, and a backup to the backup.* Course schedules often change for one reason or another. Having a Plan B and Plan C always helps.
- *Avoid Freshman courses as much as you can.* They are bigger, less personal and more difficult to get an A in. Strive for higher ranked courses, if possible. These are much smaller classes with people who tend to care more about the subject matter, and you will

be able to do much better and forge a real relationship with the professor instead of dealing with a teaching assistant.

- *Do not take no for an answer.* Let me tell a story about this one…

I had one class left to take during my spring semester in 2009, but the course was not being offered until the fall semester. Not taking that course meant I would not have the requirement completed for my second major, Philosophy. I noticed there was a graduate level course being offered in the spring semester, so I went to Professor Tony Preus and asked to be admitted to the higher level course to fulfill the requirement. He said no. I showed up again the next day. After some cajoling, I finally got him to agree to let me sit in on the first day. I ended up with a 98 on the final and an A in the class, completing my double major.

Remember, most professors teach because they love it, and because they love the students (especially the professors who have made teaching their life's work). They will often go out of their way for students who demonstrate passion. Talk to them during their office hours and explain your situation; they will listen. As a follow up to this story, I went back to Binghamton as a keynote speaker to discuss career success. The team that invited me asked me to invite a professor. You know that the Professor was Tony Preus. The circle always comes fully around!

After College

Mazal tov! You made it! What does your next adventure have in store? Graduate school perhaps? Business ownership?

How about attending grad school for free? Read on...

FREE GRADUATE SCHOOL

Yes, you read that right. You can go to graduate school for free—or at least for a fraction of the cost. Want me to show you how? (Of course you do!)

In order to get through graduate school without having to sell your kidney or taking on a quarter of a million dollars in debt, it's important to understand the landscape. The admissions test for grad school is the single most important factor in getting the school to cover your cost of attendance. Do extremely well on this test, and you're likely to get a scholarship.

It is so amazing to me how often students are willing to take on $200,000 worth in additional debt for graduate school but are unwilling to invest $1,500 in a prep program for the test. This, in my opinion, is one of the most short-sighted and asinine things imaginable.

Yes, it's true that you are brilliant and did well in college. So what? So did everyone else applying for these seats. (That's why they are called "over-achievers.") No one cares how well you did in college unless you partner your rock-star GPA with an even *more* impressive test score. The GPA is necessary, but it's not sufficient. I know the system sucks; I hate it, too. But until we can have a revolution and rid ourselves of these tests, we have to understand how to do well on them.

The best way to crack the admissions test is to take practice tests, over and over and over again. Sad but true. So if you're serious about getting ahead in grad school, get a part time job to cover the cost of the prep class and whip your ass into shape for the test. It's an investment that will save you millions of dollars over the course of your life if you do well.

Again, if you want to get a full-ride scholarship and go to grad school for free, I can't overstate the importance of this test. DO NOT WING IT!

Now let's talk about a play-by-play for pursuing different kinds of graduate degrees. I'll start with law school since that's the graduate school with which I currently have the most experience.

Law School

You get admitted to law school by taking the LSAT. The last time I checked, you must get a 162+ on the LSAT to get a full scholarship to some schools, 168+ to get into the highest ranked schools. Unless you want to be a corporate attorney at a white shoe firm (I believe these firms are going to shrink and potentially stop existing soon) go to the school that offers you the most money.

START with your END in mind

If you dream of being in Big Law, that's the only instance in which your school ranking should matter. If that's your dream, aim for the schools in the top 10-20%. The higher the school ranking, the more likely you are to get into Big Law.

Conversely, if you want to serve the public interest as an attorney and you go to an expensive school just because of its ranking, that might not make good financial sense for your future. It's great that you want to pass the torch of justice and do something for people who have no money to pay, but you can't realistically pay back your student debt on a public servant's salary. You can earn a law degree much more cheaply (or for free) and stay out of debt.

While you're in law school…

- *Do externships.* These lead to jobs. Be like the sponge and soak it all in. Real-world knowledge and expertise is learned only through practicing, not theoretical learning.
- *Take as many skills-based courses as possible.* They are more fun, and you actually learn something useful for your life. Also, getting an A+ in negotiation gives you bragging rights in any room (everyone understands that concept, and it's an incredibly useful skill). Look for courses like that.
- *Always take courses with professors who either are people who can get you jobs or who know those people.* Your baseline questions should be: If I'm a rockstar in this class, can this professor help me get a job? That's the number one requirement when picking worthwhile law classes. Adjunct professors are often a great bet because they practice law and/or are judges. Who better to hire than their star student—hopefully you?

- *Network with both lawyers and non-lawyers.* Lawyers may give you opportunities in law related fields and non-lawyers will find you impressive and will flock to you (perhaps to serve as in-house counsel for their start-up).

Your first year of law school is more important than you think.

My advice: Study for the bar exam this year. Yes, your FIRST YEAR. Every bar prep book delves heavily into first-year courses because those are what's tested on the exam. You might even get lucky and have your professors copying out of those books for their final exam questions (trust me—they do this). Study for the bar while the information is fresh in your mind.

If you can't crack the LSAT but still really, really want to be a lawyer…

I don't know what the rules are like in all states, but there is a little loophole in the New York rules for eligibility for the bar exam. In New York, you can sit for the bar if you have attended one year of law school and worked for a law firm for 4 years thereafter. Unfortunately, most people don't read this rule until they apply for the bar exam, which is usually during their last year of law school when they're already $200,000 in debt!

So with that in mind, here's an alternate strategy if you don't gain enough scholarship money from your performance on the LSAT. Instead of enrolling in law school straight away, start working for a law firm—earn some money and gain some experience. Then, negotiate with the law firm to pay for your first year of law school if you agree to work with them for an additional four. In this way, it will only take you *one year longer* to pass the bar than an evening student, and because your one year of law school is paid for and you're earning a salary the whole time, you can become an attorney with no debt, and even money in the bank! Pretty sweet gig.

If you want to go to law school but need to work to pay your other bills…

If you are capable of getting a full scholarship to law school, my advice is to go to law school full-time for the first year, then pick all evening classes for your second and third years. The advantage? You've already earned a full scholarship compared to the other students that are paying full freight at night. You will be competing against the night students for the remaining part of your law school career. Night students are a hell of a lot cooler than day students because they work jobs and are typically older. Who knows, you might even make some friends while doing it! Also, professors are a lot more lenient at night because they know everyone has been working all day, and they are usually tired at night, as well! Evening classes tend to be smaller, so there is more interaction and often an ability to do much better in the class as a result.

Getting through law school in 2.5 years

Here's another loophole for you (you're welcome). While I was a law student, I looked at the NY Court of Appeals Rules and noticed that law students have to complete six full-time semesters in order to sit for the bar exam. So I asked the Dean of Students whether I could take two part-time semesters to make a full-time equivalent, and he said yes! The solution was that I would take 6-7 credits each summer (between year 1 and 2 and between year 2 and 3), making the equivalent of one full-time semester. What did this get me? Besides graduating law school early, I also got to sit for the February bar exam. There are far fewer people who take the bar exam in February than in July, which means you get your score faster and get admitted to practice law faster.

Why does this matter? When you become a member of the bar in New York (again, I'm not sure how it is in other states—you can do the research) is that after you have passed the bar, you have to wait for a member from the ethics committee to give you an interview. This takes forever. Then, you have to wait to be slotted into a swearing-in ceremony. This can take months. This means you might have to wait a year or more after passing the bar to start practicing law! That is the sad reality of New York attorneys.

However, the February exam helps you "skip the line" and enter the marketplace at an unconventional time (remember: the anti-herd mentality wins). Also, you get to be an indentured servant to your bar review course over the winter instead of the summer, and when you walk across the stage at graduation, you walk across smiling extra big because you know you've already passed the bar while your classmates haven't even started bar prep. (Now you have an inner glimpse into my sometimes twisted mind. Don't judge!)

Other Types of Graduate Degrees

Many of the techniques I mentioned regarding law school will apply to other graduate degrees as well. For example, the better you do on your admissions test, the better your chances of getting a scholarship to cover or reduce the cost of many grad degrees. Also, you may be able to consolidate two half-time semesters to equal a full-time semester, like I did, depending on your relationships with your professors and deans. To close out this chapter, let me offer some specific advice for M.B.A. students and medical students.

Getting an M.B.A. degree

An M.B.A. is one of those grad degrees that works best when you have a bit of work experience and you go back to school for it. The M.B.A. is really an excuse to network, which means you MUST be a pro at the human interaction skills I list in the New Curriculum.

It is standard practice for your existing job to pay for your M.B.A. If it doesn't, you should only consider taking this degree if you are going to a top ranked school where you can network, and be willing to pay full freight. If that's not an option, go to a state or city school and pay a reasonable fee that won't leave you in the hole. Make sure you kill it on the admissions test in order to get as much scholarship money as possible.

Getting an M.D.

Medical school is extremely expensive. If you're pursuing an M.D., do the mathematical calculation early and often. You are looking at approximately 8 years unpaid (and taking on tremendous debt) and another 3-6 for your specialty. If helping people is the reason you are entering medicine, you may want to look into becoming a Nurse Practitioner or Physician's Assistant. There is less schooling involved, less cost and less malpractice insurance—and whatever premiums you do have to pay are usually borne by the doctor or hospital you work for. Also, if you're pursuing a career in medicine, I urge you to read the upcoming section on asset protection in detail. In my experience, medical professionals as a whole tend to leave their assets completely susceptible to creditor claims. Please, I beg you, pay attention!

Chapter 5: THE NEW CURRICULUM

Fair warning—this chapter is long. We have a lot of ground to cover.

We've spent a lot of time talking about the broken system that we call the "American Dream," and how it has devolved into a modern-day incarceration of young college students and graduates. Now it's time to introduce a different approach to education, one that focuses not just on job specialties (although those are still important), but on skills and mindsets that can lead anyone toward a richer, fuller life. I call this the NEW CURRICULUM.

The New Curriculum is a set of basic skills that unfortunately is taught nowhere. It is unacceptable that the ingredients to a successful life are not requirements in every degree conferring institution. In fact, these subjects should really be taught to students in their formative years. In my workshops and seminars around the world, we aim to give students of all ages the tools to achieve mastery of the New Curriculum.

What is this New Curriculum? Let's break it down into the following nine points, then elaborate on each of them one by one:

A. **Love Thyself and Incorporating the Millennial's Guide to the Universe**

B. **The Life Map**

C. **The Life Plan and Protecting Your Assets**

D. **The Marriage Constitution**

E. **Speaking Your Truth and Creating a New World**

F. **Scorpio Rising Means I Have Presence**

G. **"My Name Is Natalie and I Bring the Network"**

H. **Negotiate to Win**

I. **Sell Me This Pen**

A. *LOVE THYSELF*

The first requirement and the most important rule of the New Curriculum is to *love thyself*. Without this fundamental requirement met, you are doomed to a life of self-incarceration. If you do not love and understand yourself fully, you will always feel like a victim in life.

If you haven't already figured it out, I am an immensely spiritual being. Let me explain to you what I have come to understand about how we come to be who we are in this world.

Spiritually, I believe the notion that before Creation, it was just all the souls and God. These souls sat up on the assembly line and were able to pick one thing after another that would become their blemish in life, their issue that they were going to work on while in this life(time). It could be one or 100 of these different issues. Then they chose the area into which they were going to be born. That choice, is meant to perpetuate our issue/blemish and bring it to the forefront. Thereafter, our souls picked parents; then we picked our relationships, our illnesses, basically the stories of our lives. Since I came to understand this wisdom, I have become completely empowered. After all, if my world was MY choice, I KNOW that I can overcome within it.

With this in mind, it becomes clear that fear and doubt are self-imposed paradigms. We have handpicked every single issue, breakup, struggle and relationship; it's really quite comical. We picked our struggles to learn from them, but we FORGOT that we picked them! How perfectly imperfect! So what is the only thing, then, that makes this life worth living? Clearly, it is the overcoming of our hand-selected obstacles.

Think of a man who built a multibillion dollar business. His blood, sweat and tears have gone into that business. That business meant everything to that man and his family because he sacrificed for that dream. With great sacrifice, he achieved great success.

Now, what happens to most successful businesses? They slip after the founder leaves. **Why?**

As the Founder gets older, he or she starts thinking that it is time for the children to take over the business. The matriarch/patriarch puts the children in positions of power within this business, and immediately the kids became millionaires or billionaires as a result of being born to this family. And what do these sons and daughters do with what they have been given?

They (or more often their children) have a tendency of running the business into the ground.

It's true. I've witnessed this countless times in my experience as an estate attorney, looking at businesses as they transition. Time after time, the Founder's vision gets muted and the company suffers. Why?

At one time, these children chose to be born into wealthy families, so working and striving to be successful business people was not part of their DNA; it was not their unique issue that they came to this world to fix. As we all know, if you do not care about something, it certainly will not be successful. If you do not earn something, it is usually gone in the blink of an eye.

So what typically happens? The second and third generations of the family usually sink the business. The saying goes, "From T-shirts to T-shirts in three generations." The problem is that the second generation and the third generation almost always do not have the DESIRE for this business. In order to remedy this epidemic, I do a ton of business succession work with my clients to ensure that the Founders and the family that will eventually inherit the family business, are completely aligned in mission and vision of the company. Aligning the DESIRE of the multiple generations is the only way for a company to retain its success.

Therein lies the secret: Desire to BE, desire to DO, desire to ACHIEVE—these three desires form the basis of all purpose and all success. There is nothing in this world that we desire that we cannot have. In fact, it is said that if we desire it, it is meant for us. If you desire love, you are love. If you desire compassion, you are compassion, but you must earn it.

If you want the secret to success, here it is:

DESIRE + PERSPIRE = SUCCESS.

DESIRE is only step one. A simple desire in itself is not sufficient; you must WORK (PERSPIRE) for what it is you DESIRE, or else it is simply a fantasy. There is nothing you cannot do with both of these elements in place; conversely, one without the other is pointless. If you have a lot of desire but don't do any work, you will never get anything you want. If you do a lot of work with no sense of purpose and direction, you will get burnt out and hate your life and everyone in it. So it is that in the merging of the DESIRE and the HARD WORK that SUCCESS becomes a reality.

To reiterate, this book is not a magic bullet where you have the roadmap and that's it. The roadmap has always been there; it's inside of you. However, you have to travel the road. If you don't put the work in toward pursuing your desire, nothing will happen. If you don't yet understand that it's *okay* to follow your desire, even if no one else understands it (and especially so)…understand it now. You have permission. *It's okay*. This is your unique journey.

I want you to close your eyes and think of what it means to you to live your purpose. What does love feel like for you? Close your eyes and think of a white light transforming you into the person you want to be. What does it look like around you? Who is there? How do you feel? What are you doing? Are you even human anymore? This, my friends, is what it is to love thyself.

Understand that every insecurity—*I'm too fat, I'm too ugly, I'm too stupid, I'm too smart, I'm too intimidating, I'm too ridiculous, I'm too funny, I'm not funny enough, I'm too good-looking, I'm not good-looking enough*—any and all of these are simply excuses that are stopping you from living your most powerful life. My friends know that I live by this principle: NO EXCUSES, JUST TRUST!

Stop the excuses. Trust in yourself and the process. Remember:

DESIRE+PERSPIRE=SUCCESS.

You are truly living in a world that is beyond your wildest imagination. You should be completely in awe of yourself because you are walking with the Creator. When you start taking ownership of your life, the Creator and YOU become one because you are now truly in heaven. Isn't it amazing how time flies when we are with people we love, doing things we love? It's because when we walk our true path, we don't have time for the insecurities, fear and crap. Quite frankly, once we understand the deeper purpose of our work and our life, usually the focal point becomes something outside of us. In giving to something outside ourselves, we live our greatest lives. Thus, you MUST figure out clearly: What is your purpose and your desire? As I asked in Chapter 2: What is your *WHY*? My favorite moment in our seminars is to watch people figure that out. Once you have figured it out, as the great Ms. Britney Spears says: It's time to "Work, Bitch!"

B. *THE LIFE MAP*

If we can all think back to Alice in Wonderland, we know that Alice has a conversation with the Chesire cat about getting to her destination. However, Alice does not really care what destination she is trying to get to. The Chesire Cat, then, profoundly states "then it doesn't matter which way you go…you are sure too get somewhere…if you only walk long enough".

When figuring out the steps we need to take in order to achieve "*SUCCESS*," like Alice in the illustration above, we need to understand where we are going. This is why in our New Curriculum seminars we go through an intense life mapping session, complete with vision boards, fun and (sometimes) glitter. The resulting life map becomes our internal GPS that should guide each and every decision we make in our lives. Anything that does not fit in with our goals should be immediately discarded.

For the purposes of this book, let me give you a taste of the kinds of questions you'll need to ask yourself in order to figure out where your life map leads.

1. *What do you do every day that makes you lose track of time?*

2. *What are your favorite hobbies?*

3. *How do you choose to spend your weekends?*

4. *If you could think of an ideal life, what would it look like?*

5. *Which people do you admire most?*

6. *What is it about those people that you admire?*

7. *If you were told you had 3 years to live, how would you spend your time?*

8. *If you were told you had 3 months to live, how would you spend your time?*

9.   *What are the problems in the world that keep you up at night?*

10.   *What one accomplishment do you treasure most?*

11.   *What was your defining moment in your life that changed everything?*

12.   *What would you do for no payment?*

The answers to these questions will help you ascertain what it is you truly want in life, and you can use them to help your form your life map. In the New Curriculum training, we also delve into many more questions and have our clients take assessment tests such as Myers-Brigg and the DISC personality test. These tests usually provide a good gauge to reveal the natural strengths of each individual.

Your life map should focus on your strengths—and for that matter, so should your life itself. If we focus on things we love and are naturally good at, we as people are more likely to be successful in our endeavors.

C. THE LIFE PLAN and PROTECTING YOUR ASSETS

Once you have developed your life map and done your vision board, you need to get your ducks in a row. I'm talking specifically about your financial and legal readiness to take the leap and lead the life you want. It might seem a bit odd to talk about financial planning as part of the New Curriculum, but trust me—it matters. No matter how old-school it might seem, the estate planning paradigm is still the most important foundation you need in order to ensure everything you are building does not disintegrate like a house built on sand.

The major problem with estate planning, which is my area of legal expertise, is that it scares the bejeezus out of people! "What do you mean I am going to die? Me! Die?! Never!" (As if we are going to make it out of this thing alive.)

Because people don't want to face their own mortality, they often never get around to planning for it in the first place. Some studies show that as many as 64% of people pass away without a will. It's understandably scary to grapple with the questions like *What happens if I die or if I become incapacitated?* So in order to not think about it, people simply put their heads in the sand and hope that the angel of death will forget about them. Good luck with that! How can people be so reckless with their life savings that they fail to decide how it will be divvied up? How can parents be so short-sighted that they don't specify who would take care of their minor children in the event of untimely death?

It is completely irresponsible, and the reason it is never done is because it's not mandated. I propose that this scary topic actually be embraced as a necessary step to live a truly meaningful and purposeful life! After all, how can you fully live authentically if you are always nervous that your family won't be taken care of because you (willingly) forgot to plan?

Here are the absolute must-knows and must-haves for every person with a pulse. (I'm pretty sure if you are reading this, that means you.)

Set Up Your Beneficiaries Properly

The following accounts should have the correct beneficiaries attached. Do not assume that this has been properly done. Make sure!

- Life insurance policies
- Checking and savings accounts
- 401(k)
- IRA
- Roth IRA
- Any military benefits
- Trusts (make sure the trust document is up to date)
- Deeds (please look at what your deed says and do not assume!)
- Investments (e.g., stocks and bonds)

Please understand that even if you have a will, the beneficiary designations on the above documents will take precedence over your will. To illustrate this, let me share some terrible true stories with you:

STORY #1: A thirty-eight-year-old woman became a widow. Her loving husband had requested paperwork to have his life insurance changed from his mother to his wife. Then, he simply forgot to submit the paperwork to the company and died. Before he was buried, his mother had cashed in the policy as his current beneficiary. The widow was left penniless, childless and alone.

STORY #2: A twenty-five-year-old woman walked into a financial advisor's office because she knew that her newly deceased mother had visited her. It turned out the deceased woman had not actually hired the financial advisor, but this advisor took sympathy on the young woman and made some calls on her behalf anyway. She found that there was a two-million-dollar life insurance policy, but when the advisor gave the company the daughter's name, it did not match as the beneficiary listed on the policy.

After much cajoling, the insurance company told the advisor who was listed as the beneficiary: It was a man's name that the daughter didn't immediately recognize. The next day, the daughter came back and said she believed the man was a former fiancé of her mother's. They had never gotten married, which meant the divorce law that otherwise would have severed the beneficiary designation never went into effect. The advisor and the daughter traced the man's information and told him the story, expecting the best.

What they got was a heavy dose of reality.

"She was the love of my life and she broke my heart…I'm keeping the money," he said. Just like that, this man received every dollar that this woman intended to leave as a legacy to her daughter.

Fair? No.

Legal? Yes.

Lesson? Clean up your beneficiary designations and check them thrice.

Get Your Documents in Order

There is zero excuse not to do this. Get at least the following basic documents in order: ***Power of Attorney, Will*** and ***Healthcare Proxy.*** If you are over eighteen, this means you. It doesn't matter if you have no assets; you must do this. Work out a payment plan with the attorney if you have to. Better yet, see the end of this section where I offer a cost-effective alternative. However you choose to do it, get this covered!

Let's go over the basic documents one by one.

Power of Attorney

What happens to your legal and financial obligations if something happens to you that leaves you unable to uphold those obligations? There are plenty of potential issues here that could leave you incapacitated, including early onset Alzheimer's disease, a coma resulting from an auto accident and others.

The fact that you've been rendered incapable of handling those matters doesn't mean they go away. Someone will need to attend to them. That's where your power of attorney (POA) comes in. The person designated as your POA is responsible for handling financial and legal matters if you are unable to do so. Both you and your spouse should have a power of attorney assigned; optimally, you should each name the other as your POA. (If you divorce, you would most likely want to change your power of attorney to someone other than your ex-spouse.) Note that your power of attorney is only valid as long as you live. Once you die, the person designated in this document has no control over your estate or its assets.

There are three different types, or variations, of the power of attorney. The most common type, and the one that works best in most cases, is a *durable power of attorney*. This POA is valid the instant the paperwork is signed and will go into effect immediately if you are declared mentally incompetent. The second type is called a *springing power of attorney*; this will take effect if you are seriously injured or become seriously ill. The third variation is called a *non-durable power of attorney* and is used if you need someone to stand in your place in a legal or financial matter and are unable to attend to it yourself. For instance, if you're closing on a house but are on the other side of the country and can't make the signing, your designated POA can take your place.

Your Will

Yes, we need to discuss your will—that is, both your will and that of your spouse. Remember, all of us will die. Having a will does not mean you are preparing to die. *Living* means you are preparing to die. No, you're not too young. No one should be without a will, particularly if you're married and are starting a family or if you have any assets. Accidents and disease can strike at any age, and if you die without a will in place, you'll have no say in what happens to your things, who will care for your children, etc.

For example, if you were to die and your sister was the closest living relative to your children, there's a good chance the court will appoint her as their guardian, whether she's the one you wanted to name or not. The same thing applies to assets you own – without a will in place, it's up to the court to determine where those go after your death.

Your will specifies exactly what goes to whom, who will care for your minor children and a great deal more. It's an incredibly important document, and everyone (married or not) needs to have one. However, there are a few things that you need to know ahead of time that will affect your planning and the process.

First, you'll need witnesses to the signing of the will. This can be anyone you choose, but understand that legally your witnesses should not be beneficiaries to the will.

You'll also need to give some thought to whom you will name as the executor—the person responsible for executing your will after your death. He or she will be in charge of carrying out your wishes in terms of property division, but also for paying any taxes due on your estate, as well as other tasks.

Finally, if you have children, you'll need to name a guardian. (I recommend naming a couple, if possible.) You want to give this choice some careful consideration because these people could be responsible not only for feeding and clothing your children until they turn 18, but also for raising them, teaching them and caring for them for possibly many years. Please make sure whomever you name is prepared to stand in that position. Let them know beforehand that you are slotting them for this position, and have a conversation about how you want your children to be raised. I met a young man once whose guardians (aunt and uncle) had no idea what to do with him. As a result, he ended up in foster care. Please do not allow this to happen to your beloved child. It's scary to plan, but it is even scarier to leave this up to chance, the courts and the foster care system.

If you have (or will have) adult children who are not capable of living on their own due to health or mental concerns, then you'll need to establish a supplemental needs trust (also called a special needs trust) for them. Again, this is something you'll need to consider very carefully since children in this situation might need lifelong care.

The people you choose for these positions will literally either define your legacy or completely screw it up. Please choose wisely, but please CHOOSE. If it is not perfect, that's okay; it can always be changed. Do not let the lack of a so-called perfect candidate stop you from making the decision. In the event of the demise of you and your spouse, the court won't have the luxury of figuring out the perfect person. It is better for you to decide than a judge who has no idea about your family dynamics.

Healthcare Proxy

Planning for the future means confronting some difficult concepts, things that none of us really wants to think about. For instance, what happens if you're involved in a car accident and go into a coma? What happens if you're in a permanent vegetative state? What happens if this should occur to your spouse?

If something like this happens to you, you will not be in any condition to make decisions about your care, its quality, or any other areas of your life. This is why you need a healthcare proxy, along with what's called a living will. Really, a healthcare proxy is nothing more than a legal document that names an agent who can make decisions regarding your medical care if you are unable to do so. Obviously, this should be someone you trust and who knows your wishes if certain situations should arise. Your spouse is usually the most obvious choice. For students reading this- you MUST have these documents. Once you turn 18, your parents are no longer your guardians!

There are two situations in which such an agent may be necessary. The first is in a temporary situation where you're unable to make decisions regarding your own medical care. For example, you're knocked unconscious, or you're under general anesthesia and incapable of responding to questions or making decisions, but only for a limited time. In this instance, your agent would be responsible for making decisions that involve unanticipated situations that occur while you're in this condition. Once you regain consciousness, your agent's role is done.

The second situation involves a permanent inability to make decisions regarding your medical care, such as a prolonged coma or vegetative state. Here is where the living will comes in. Your living will should be a list of your wishes about medical treatments (or the lack thereof) should certain situations come to pass. For instance, it would deal with your wishes about ongoing medical care should you be in a permanent vegetative state. A living will communicates your desires to your agent, to your primary care physician and others. It may also apply if you were rendered incapable of communicating (although still conscious) or if you were suffering from Alzheimer's or another form of dementia. In these instances, your agent would be responsible for making all of your medical care decisions.

In either instance, your agent acts as your voice—a stand-in for you, yourself. That means your agent should know very well what your actual choice would be and not be guided by his/her own desires.

The combination of naming an agent and creating a living will constitutes your advanced directive—the expression of your desires in the anticipation that you might not be able to do so later. Chances are good that you will name your spouse as your healthcare agent, and there's nothing wrong with this. However, you need to make sure that you're both on the same page about medical care if you are incapacitated, particularly if you are permanently unable to communicate.

These three documents—the power of attorney, the will and the healthcare proxy—are non-negotiable. They are a must for each and every person! Trusts are not mandatory, but they are often extremely beneficial. Let's turn our attention now to what trusts are and why we need them.

Trusts

There are many types of trusts, and chances are good that you may not be familiar with all of them. The type that is most important to this discussion is called a *revocable living trust*. It works in conjunction with your will and helps you avoid the problem of probate. All wills must be probated, but you can title your assets to go to a living trust instead, saving both time and money.

When your assets are held in a revocable living trust, they will not go through probate when you die; the trust transfers them directly to your chosen beneficiaries. The alternative is that your estate spends months, perhaps years, in the probate process, during which time the costs may rise to as much as 5% of the total estate's value. With a large estate, that's quite a lot of money lost that could have been saved by a trust.

There are quite a few other benefits to revocable living trusts, many of which are due to the "revocable" nature of these instruments. One of the most important things to understand is that these trusts can be amended over time, which allows you to change things as needed. A few other benefits to mention:

- A living trust is private (by contrast, a will is public);

- You can continue to use the assets in the trust during your lifetime;

- The trust is active immediately;

- The trust allows you to set aside assets for a child without endangering the child's right to public benefits;

- A successor trustee of your own choosing takes over administration after you die;

- You can provide directions to the successor trustee to ensure that your wishes are carried out even after your death; and

- After your death, the living trust becomes an irrevocable trust.

While a living trust is an important tool that offers quite a bit of protection, it is not a replacement for a will. Only a will can name a guardian for minor children, for example. Thus, a trust should only be considered as an addition to a will, not as a substitute for it.

On the other end of the spectrum are *irrevocable trusts*. These differ significantly from living trusts in two important ways: First, they cannot be changed easily without the beneficiary's permission (something that does not apply to living trusts); and second, you give up any rights to the assets transferred into the trust, and you lose the ability to use those assets (with some loopholes, of course). Once they're in the trust, they will go to the beneficiary upon your death. Sometimes it is possible to change the terms of an irrevocable trust, but it requires you to obtain permission from the trustee, as well as everyone else involved, and it is not a simple process. This also usually comes with hefty fees.

Why would anyone want to set up an irrevocable trust when it's possible to use a living trust? There are several reasons why this might be a better choice for you, particularly if there's a need to reduce the worth of your taxable estate. You cannot save any money by putting assets into a revocable trust as the IRS basically doesn't recognize revocable trusts for tax purposes. This is because you technically retain control of all the assets in the trust. In an irrevocable trust, you're essentially giving up control of those assets permanently, effectively removing them from your taxable estate.

It's important to note that irrevocable trusts offer the most tax advantages to those with a considerable amount of wealth. However, that doesn't mean they can't also be a valuable tool for those less well off. They can help provide a guaranteed source of support for disabled dependents, or they can be used to protect personal assets against professional liability. That said, you'll need to weigh the surrender of control over those assets against the benefits you gain from an irrevocable trust.

Asset Protection

Trusts are the number one source for asset protection. In fact, in our long history as a people, trusts have been used by every (smart) wealthy family for generations. Asset protection is of extreme importance. I am not impressed by how much a person makes, but rather by their understanding of how what they make could be taken from them. Lawyers and greedy people who see anyone with wealth as a "deep pocket" are really to blame for this epidemic. You could be minding your own business and get hit by a lawsuit just because you happened to be in the wrong place at the wrong time, or just because someone wants to force a settlement from you, even if you've done nothing wrong.

This is a far too familiar experience. Courts are being weighed down by the number of ridiculous claims judges have to hear. Everyone thinks that they can just sue, sue, sue, and this society in America absolutely encourages lawsuits. How do you ensure that your hard-earned dollars aren't taken by creditors, predators, divorcing spouses, taxes or lawsuits?

First, do your asset protection planning *before* there is a problem. If you wait until after there's a problem or a claim against your wealth, you have done what is called a fraudulent conveyance that will not be upheld in a court of law.

Second, you need to weigh your own assets against the need for advanced planning. Are you going into a practice area where litigation is rampant? Are you super wealthy and afraid of the tax ramifications if you don't have the right planning in place? What about insurance? How much do you carry, and are you under-insured?

These are all important questions to ask a qualified professional. However, the most important global things to understand are the following:

1. *Estate taxes are astronomical.* You would be foolish not to plan around this and ensure that to the greatest extent possible, the government does not become the majority

stakeholder in your life's work. (LLCs, trusts and discounting methods mixed with life insurance often work for this aim.)

2. *If you're getting married and are worried about a spouse becoming a creditor, make sure there is a trust in place.* You can even put your spouse in as a trustee. Make sure that the spouse can easily be fired in the event of a divorce. This is in addition to a prenuptial agreement, and unlike a prenup, it is much harder to contest.

3. *If you own rental property, make sure your property is properly insured and that your renters have their own insurance.* Also, make sure the property is held in the name of an LLC or trust to sanctify it and separate it from the rest of your assets. How terrible would it be if your renter's friend that was injured on your property could sue you for everything you are worth because you owned the house in your personal name?

4. *Long term care costs are astronomical.* You should consider purchasing a long-term care policy immediately. I've had coverage on myself since I was 25. It is cheap at this age and is an absolute must! Imagine having to spend $25,000/month in care in your last few years. This expense has wiped out many of my clients financially, and I do not want to see it happen to any future generations.

5. *If you are in a high-risk business, do not even think of putting your personal name on any of the assets.* Everything you own should be in the name of a trust or LLC.

One more thing before we leave this topic: In order to alleviate the process and the legal fee it costs, I built a system called Will On Command. This system is an affordable, accessible and automated process to make the estate planning process available to all people, regardless of how much money they have. You can get an estate plan at www.willoncommand.com.

D. THE MARRIAGE CONSTITUTION

Marriage – it's an incredibly exciting experience. You're about to embark on a new life with someone you can't imagine not spending all of your time with. It's a joining of two separate people into a single entity, the chance to start a family and more. It's also a huge commitment that hopefully will last for life. Something this important should be documented so both spouses understand the expectations each brings into the relationship. This is why I highly recommend drafting a marriage constitution.

Now, we have already discussed the financial considerations that must occur in order for each person to be financially protected. To reiterate, both persons in a couple must each have a will, power of attorney and health care proxy. They should also consider buying their family home in the name of a trust.

This discussion goes way beyond a prenuptial agreement and who gets what in the event of a divorce. Although financial implications are of course discussed through the marriage constitution drafting process (which is a facilitated discussion with a trained facilitator), they are secondary to the most pressing reasons that marriages crumble.

The true intention of the marriage constitution is to ensure that a divorce doesn't occur. So what does a marriage constitution actually entail? I call the discussion points for the marriage constitution the GREAT EIGHT PILLARS OF MARITAL SUCCESS.

1. *List of financial assets and liabilities.* So many marriages end because of a spouse not being open and honest about this. This must be discussed because it is an absolute requirement to ensure that a couple has the best chance possible of making it.

2. *Sex.* How often is it going to happen? This might seem strange to discuss when you can't keep your hands off each other at this point, but believe me, it is extremely important to discuss in detail to ensure that your baseline expectations are understood. Is three times a week our minimum expectation? Maybe we want to have one week off each month so that we always miss each other (a version of this is apparent in Judaism; it's called *niddah*). The point is, it's individual to each couple, but it should be discussed before a couple gets married so that there is a clear understanding between each party and no surprises as to what the expectations actually are.

3. *Vacations.* How many vacations is the family going to take during the year? Are they all with kids? How much money will this couple allocate to vacations each year? If it

gets managed, it matters. If vacations matter to a couple, they should be planned for and budgeted.

4. *Dates.* How many date nights will you have a month? This is imperative if you want to have a happy marriage. After all, once the flirtation and excitement is gone, so too can the marriage quickly disintegrate.

5. *Family.* Do you want a family? How many kids? Where will they go to school? What community will they be part of? Is there money for extracurricular activities? What are the values we want to bestow on these children? How often will our respective parents have access to the children? These are all extremely important questions to answer as a familial unit if you truly want to maximize your chances of living a happy marriage and building a loving family.

6. *Community.* What community are you a part of, and which communities will you continue to be a part of once the marriage happens? Are boys/girls nights allowed? Which religious organizations will you be a part of? Is philanthropy important to you?

7. *Body.* Are tattoos allowed? Piercings? Extra-marital sex? This is not meant to be a judgment but simply a mutual understanding to ensure that each of the partners understands the parameters and ground rules of the marriage.

8.	*Blueprint*. What is the blueprint for each of your lives, and can you easily integrate them together? Something will have to be sacrificed or accommodated. What will it be? Who will cook for the kids? Who will take them to school? Whose career is going to take a hit? Are nannies allowed? Tutors? Do you believe the kids can be educated at multiple different places, or is having one static school important to you? These are all things that must be hashed out before the marriage occurs to maximize the chance of success.

E. *SPEAKING YOUR TRUTH and CREATING A NEW WORLD*

Our words are the most important thing we have. Our words literally define how we show up in the world, and for a large part, define how successful we will be. If we can easily articulate our point through the spoken language, we can absolutely shift reality and effectively market ourselves and our companies. Also, being a master with words allows us to receive job offer after job offer. That is truly how important the spoken word is.

It's a shame to see how many people are terrible communicators, and technology hasn't made it easier. In fact, it's probably made it a lot harder. Everywhere we go, we are confronted with statements that Millennials are terrible communicators and do not understand how to speak and interact with others. Thanks in part to social media and our smartphones, people have literally become so numb to real human interaction that they are petrified of making a mistake or sounding stupid in public. As a result, they stay at home on the Internet or get wasted at parties to lessen the implications of a misspoken word.

This is an unsettling and completely unacceptable cultural norm. Having the ability to speak passionately about who you are, and what your vision is—this is absolutely vital for international dreamers and for the new Millennial rockstar.

Most people's biggest fear in life is public speaking. (The second biggest fear is death.) This means many of us would rather be in the casket than giving the eulogy. That's outrageous!

Public speaking can no longer be an option; it must become a social and educational requirement, and it must happen early and often! Furthermore, social interaction classes are necessary to ensure that people are able to coalesce with other similar minded people. Again, it is in the collective WE that true shifts can happen in the world. Our spoken and written word, though, must be integrated as basic requirements for success in the new frontier, the new Information Age we are currently entering.

F. SCORPIO RISING MEANS YOU HAVE PRESENCE. (Presence Means You Win.)

Any juvenile astrologist will tell you that I am an Aries, Scorpio rising. What does this mean for those of you who have no idea about the zodiac? Simply put, your rising sign is how the world sees you. Scorpio rising means that I have presence. Presence, or at least how I define it, is the ability to walk into a room and be noticed, to command attention and respect immediately.

In Amy Cuddy's book *Presence*, she states that presence is the state of being able to comfortably express our true thoughts, feelings, values, talents and knowledge. She further describes it as knowing who you are and being able to access that person when you most need to. Presence, in my humble opinion, is one of the most important skills a person can have. Although many people believe that presence is something you are born with or not (as in Scorpio rising), it is certainly something that can be taught. For more information on how you can try to become more present, I would highly suggest referring to Amy Cuddy's book and reading on her power posing techniques.

Presence has a lot to do with confidence and self-esteem. How you present yourself in a group is how you are etched into a person's mind. That presentation, and the initial perception of your ability to command a room, make the difference between people asking you to be on their board, a speaker for their panel or their business partner, or simply looking at you as a kid who needs them for a job or internship. That's how truly powerful your self-perception emanates out into the world, and it is what I call presence.

When I was twenty-four years old and had just started my law firm, I had a lot of bravado and presence. I didn't have much else. I didn't come from a wealthy family. I didn't know much at the time, but I knew that working like an indentured servant so that someone else could grow rich was not why I became a lawyer. So, naturally, I decided to start my own firm.

I knew my area of practice and was lucky enough to team up with some wonderful people simply because of my courage to walk into the room. While I was considering starting my own law firm, yet still a miserable peon working in a mill of a law firm (as most of them are), I put in a resume to a leading life insurance firm.

From their perspective, I had an awesome resume. To them, I was a young, hungry trusts and estates female lawyer. They called me immediately, and I had a meeting with the recruiting chair on Monday. After speaking to him for 20 minutes, I bluntly told him that I didn't want to be an insurance agent. Rather, I wanted him to introduce me to the powers that be so that I could become the in-house draftsperson attorney in the office. (This was one of the leading offices in the country for life insurance sales.)

The recruiting manager took a liking to me and walked me into the managing partner's office immediately. I pitched him. He loved it. He was a Mets fan; I was a lawyer from Queens. Sometimes it literally just takes the balls to ask, and the confidence to strut into the managing partner's office, to make it happen.

I didn't end up going internally into that firm; what I did get was something much bigger. The managing partner invited me in to meet with his top insurance agent, a man who had been with the company for 34 years and was a leading expert nationwide. He asked me if I knew who he was. I courageously said that I had looked him up on the company website, and that's all the information I knew about him. He stated that he was the king of estate planning, and that he would do one better for me then bringing me internally. He then introduced me to one of the top estate lawyers in the country.

Before I knew it, I was on a plane to meet this attorney. From these men, in the first year of my career, I learned more about sophisticated estate planning than 90% of other attorneys in the field. Furthermore, I now had resources and the "back office" to call if I ever had a complex situation arise.

So often, when I speak to younger people encouraging them to live their dream, I find they have been taught that they do not have enough experience. What if they don't know something? What if they make a mistake?

The truth is, we all make mistakes. Hopefully, those mistakes are not so big that we can't remedy them once they are made. Also, as long as we know the right people to call—people with expertise who are in our corner—we have a safety net of sorts. It's the same notion as a young associate bringing business into a firm and having a managing partner send down the work to a qualified attorney. The experienced and seasoned people usually really suck at getting business and bringing in the dollars; they rely on young and hungry people to make that happen.

In fact, I submit that the younger person in the transaction of any business is actually the one doing a lot more work. Here's why. In law, medicine, investment banking, marketing, whatever the hell you choose to do with your time, it's not rocket science (unless it is, in which case you *are* a rocket scientist and this is what you do, so the point still remains). Once you've done it once or twice or five times, the pattern doesn't change all that much. You might have a client with a nuanced family issue or a new disruptor company you haven't worked with yet, but the truth is 99% of the issues are the same, time and time again.

So if technology is getting so good that it can replace technical know-how, it seems that experience and age are no longer a factor because the technology system has taken care of that. Therefore, the *presence* and *confidence* factors are truly one's most important assets when it comes to starting a business or being a rainmaker for an existing business.

You kill what you eat in the world of entrepreneurship. However, killing what you eat does NOT necessarily mean you network like a hunter. Networking and getting people to like you is a lot more like farming then hunting. Let me explain that difference…

G. *"MY NAME IS NATALIE AND I BRING THE NETWORK"*

In junior high school, we would usually do an icebreaker on the first day of classes. I don't know about you all, but my teachers loved to play the picnic icebreaker. You would have to introduce yourself by your first name, and using the same first letter of your first name, you would pick a utensil or something of the sort you would bring to the picnic.

My first name is Natalie. What could Natalie possibly bring to the picnic that started with an "N" except for napkins? Please tell me if anyone figures out a better "N" word for picnic appropriate stuff. I really abhorred being relegated to bringing the napkins all the time. Napkins are weak. They clean up the mess after all the fun has been had, and if you know anything about me, I'm not a cleaner sort. I like to be in the middle of the party. Actually, scratch that: I *am* the party.

With that notion in mind, I finally smile whenever this cursed memory of napkin bringing comes up because now...

I'M NATALIE, AND I BRING THE NETWORK.

Here's a secret: I don't care what letter your name starts with. If you are the person who can bring the network, people always want to be around you. Own this point for yourself: Replace my name with yours. "My name is _____ and I bring the network."

If you have a network, number one, you are probably a cool and well liked person with good hygiene. Number two, you probably know how to work a room. Again, if we learned anything from presence, the working-the-room factor is probably the single most important asset for any aspiring partners of existing firms or entrepreneurs to have.

Networks are undeniably important and valuable—just look at Facebook's valuation as a social network. Networks are why the Kardashians, and any celebrity influencer, for that matter, makes the money they make. If one of these people says something good about your product, other people are more willing to buy it.

Do you understand that you have that power yourself? Why are testimonials so important? Why do people love word-of-mouth networking? Why do people judge us based on what other people say? It's simply because this is the intrinsic value we as humans have placed on other people's opinions.

Now, imagine if a big corporations—paid for an event for you to speak. I'm talking thousands of dollars in overhead, all covered for you to give a presentation just so that your network can be present. Guess what? It's done everyday and I'm often asked to give such a presentation.

But why me?

Very simple: Word got around that I have a huge and very influential network. This is a network I started building as a kid in high school, then continuing into college and in my professional life. If you bring the network, people will pay big money to access it. Your contacts are gold.

Now, I'm not suggesting that people should put a bid on your contacts and want to hang out with you for that reason alone. What I am saying is that any truly successful person who has made it, particularly if they have a role in the company to bring in sales, necessarily must have a strong network. A strong network is what differentiates "B" lawyers and brokers from superstars, and why people spend thousands, if not millions, of dollars a year to be part of the right clubs, organizations, charitable organizations and schools.

Your network DEFINES how much MONEY you make.

So, life lesson: Start networking right now. If you are a student and not involved in clubs and organizations on campus, you are wasting your time. That statute or rule of economics or whatever you are studying for homework can be Googled in 1.5 seconds; don't waste too much time on it. Your contact making abilities are strongest when you are young because people look at the length of time of a relationship to evaluate how strong it is. If you are hanging out in the library all day and getting B-pluses, stop. You probably aren't that great at school and would do much better for your life building a robust network!

The truth is, good students will always be good with very little work. You probably can't beat them there. However, whether you're a good student or not, you can shine socially, and I'm willing to bet if you outshine the "A students" socially, and you may actually do much better than your peers. MUCH BETTER. It's not a competition, but if you are going to be living already, wouldn't you prefer to live well, rather than working tortuously to make someone else wealthy who doesn't even see your skill set? Don't do it!

Always have your finger on the pulse of your city and know what is going on. The company you work for is one bad deal away from bankruptcy, and you're trusting them to take care of you? Wake up. Don't wait until you are out of a job to start networking because people can smell the desperation. Also, don't you dare bring a resume to a networking function. You are not there to apply for a job—you are there to bring value for the other people in the room. If you do that, believe me, they will pay you back ten-fold over time.

Hunting versus Farming

The people who go to networking events trying to close business that night or get a job are the biggest losers I've ever met. That's not what networking is. That's what I call the *hunter networker*—the kind of person who seeks contacts as if they were prey. The hunter networker might as well be a sleazy, overweight used car salesman who is trying to have sex with you on the first date.

Don't think like a hunter when you're networking; instead, think like a farmer. The *farmer networker* sees his network as a field to be cultivated. Sow seeds. Water them. Pull weeds. Nurture. Cultivate. In time, those contacts will bring you a great harvest.

Networking is the exchange of value to another person. You want this exchange to be worthy enough for them to remember who you are and want to do business with you in the future.

Networking is a lot like dating. If you ask someone for their business the first time you meet, it's like still being at the restaurant on the first date and getting them undressed. It doesn't work, it might get you smacked, and it will certainly ruin your reputation.

Any meaningful relationship is built in steps through experiences. So too, is networking. You cannot expect someone you have met once to refer you their number one client. How could they? Their credibility is on the line every time they make a referral. Typically, a person has to be in contact with you at least six times in order to feel secure enough to send you a referral. There are ways to speed this process up, which I discuss in my seminars worldwide.

Networking is about karma. When you give openly and graciously, when you connect others for no benefit of your own, the universe conspires to make sure you get what you need. (Usually it comes from an unrelated source). That's just how networking works, and it takes time.

I have served as the president of a networking organization that has an international presence. Our job is to give business to our fellow members. By being part of this network, I have been able to close on hundreds of thousands of dollars of new business and made some of my dearest friends. Hopefully, you are starting to see how powerful your network can be.

Super powerful networkers are called *connectors*. A connector is a person who sees how two or more other people need to meet to grow their businesses. A connector as a contact can literally change your business. In case you are wondering, I am a connector and a raving fan of connectors. If I love you, the entire city will know it. I have personally transformed multiple businesses because I do not shut up about things and experiences I LOVE!

Nine Fine Networking Nuggets

Some key points to remember regarding networking:

1. *Your network is gold.* Guard your network and make sure you protect them from unscrupulous people.

2. *Start networking early and often.*

3. *If you are well networked, you will be successful.* Period.

4. *Don't rely solely on your job for your network.* That business could be bankrupt tomorrow.

5. *Never bring a resume to a networking event* (or risk me finding out and smacking you).

6. *Always look to give business first.* The universe will conspire to make sure you always get it back. (This is the Law of Attraction in its most basic form.)

7. *Don't try to sell someone on your services at the initial meeting.* (To reiterate, it's like sex in public on a first date, and even in this Tinder age, it is completely inappropriate).

8. *Always keep connectors close.*

9. *Be interesting and always well dressed, smelling fantastic.*

A Few more Bonus Tips. If you want to be the next Millennial Networking Master of the Universe, do the following:

1. *Join or start organizations that meet regularly.* Once a month is the absolute minimum; twice a month is better.

2. *If you are a student or work at a company, join a team, club, sorority, fraternity or league.* This is where you will make your friends and networks that last a lifetime.

3. *Start your own events.* A networker is great, but the leader of a network is the most valuable. Network leaders are connectors.

4. *Become a connector and start being grateful for others.* Just watch how this will change not only your business, but also your life. You reap what you sow.

H. *NEGOTIATE TO WIN*

Negotiation is one of the most important skills to have in order to live a long and fulfilling life. Why? *Life is a negotiation.* Your interactions with your parents, professors, spouse, students and children are all forms of negotiation. We have been negotiating for things since we were little. However, so few of us actually get to refine that skill that most of us just wing it.

In law school, I was one of twenty kids who was lucky enough to get into the negotiation class that was offered once a year. I ended up getting an A+ in that class and thereafter became the teaching assistant and coach for all future negotiation teams. Can you believe that each year, only 20 people in a law school get to understand how to negotiate? We are talking about lawyers who get paid to be alleged expert negotiators and negotiate on behalf of other people, yet so few of them have ever been trained in this art!

So what is negotiation? Negotiation does not mean domineering the other side and stuffing them into a position they do not want to be in. For a negotiation to be truly successful, it must be mutually beneficial for each of the parties, every time.

I used to be a hard ball negotiator who prided myself on getting the best deals. I used to smile knowing I had just taken the person on the other side of the table for everything they had. Then, I began to notice that no one wanted to negotiate against me because I had a reputation as a bull dog.

While it might work to be a bull dog for a one-off negotiation, most negotiations are done in the context of a lasting relationship. For these to work, it truly has to be a win-win scenario. Once the parties stop trusting each other, the entire deal is in danger of falling apart.

Here are some of my most important negotiation tips:

1. *Never make the first offer unless you are in the position of having the most knowledge, and it is customary in said transactions for your "side" to make the offer.* For example, if you are the employer, it is customary for you to make the initial offer of a job.

2. *Always know who is across the table.* Know their name, where they grew up, what they like, what culture they are part of. These are all helpful clues to help you get them to like you. Likability is everything! People generally only do business with people they know, like and trust. Without all of these things present, a deal will not get done no matter how attractive the figures might be. Many business deals have soured because something didn't "feel" right. Some of the most successful business people are super spiritual and listen to their intuition about other people. So understanding the questions above and tapping into that person's security and trust will absolutely put you in a position to get a deal done.

3. *Never jump right into business.* Rapport is required first. Without building up rapport you are effectively jumping into bed before taking someone on a first date. (I know I keep making this point, but I want to drive it home.) Don't do it! You will lose each and every time. On this point, also be especially sensitive to a person's culture. An American is much more willing to get to business quickly as opposed to someone from Japan, for example, who likes to take his time and is very indirect with his contact.

4. *Be hard on the issues and soft on the people.* In their book *Getting to Yes: Negotiating Agreement Without Giving In*, Roger Fisher and William Ury make this exact point. It is just as relevant today as it was in 1983 when the book was published. The negotiation is not personal and should never get contentious. When you build rapport with people, it is a lot less likely to become a contested and heated discussion. This doesn't mean that you should give in to anything that does not best serve your purpose; in fact, you should not accept anything that does not serve you. However,

this is not the same as getting angry at the person across the table. It is not personal. Remember, they must also not be willing to accept anything that does not serve them.

5. *Quit positional bargaining and get to the heart of the issue.* Again, in *Getting to Yes,* the authors discuss the scenario of an orange to illustrate positional negotiation. Two brothers want one orange and are arguing with each other over it. They are practically in fists when their mother interjects, asking each brother *why* he needs the orange. One brother says he wants to make juice from the insides of the orange; the other needs the orange peels for jam. It becomes clear that "needing the entire orange" is in fact a *position*. Once the mother understood the heart of the issue and the underlying interests, she gave the inside to one and the peel to the other, satisfying both. The Moral: Asking *why* someone across the table wants something is key to successful negotiations because it moves past each person's *position* to the motive behind it, opening the door for win-win solutions.

6. *Do your research and know your alternatives.* This is all about leverage. If you have no better option, you need to be willing to take a deal and be more flexible with your terms. If you have four other offers on the table, you can absolutely flex your negotiation muscles at the table.

7. *Be cognizant of the sex of the negotiating party.* For whatever reason, women are still considered "bossy" if they negotiate from a position of strength, while men negotiating from the same position are seen as capable and confident. The research tells an unfortunate story, but a true one nonetheless, that women will often do better at the table by advocating that they have to do this on behalf of some greater thing outside themselves.

8. *Always be prepared.* This goes without saying, but you must know your facts and figures cold. Don't rely on PowerPoint; in fact, I would suggest not even bringing technology into the room. Face-to-face negotiation is much more beneficial for the prepared party as opposed to the other.

9. *Lose the battle, win the war.* Keep in mind that this transaction is presumably a long-term contract or relationship of some sort. Sometimes, it is better to lose the battle and win the war—to give up something in the short term for greater outcomes later. Remember, reputations take a lifetime to build and seconds to destroy.

I. SELL ME THIS PEN

In the closing scene of *Wolf of Wall Street*, Leonardo DiCaprio's character Jordan Belfour instructs his seminar attendees, "Sell me this pen." What he was asking them to do was *create a need* for the pen. When you create a need in the customer, the sale is already made, no matter the price—assuming, of course, that you've pre-qualified the buyer to afford the item. (You are not going to sell a Porsche to someone who makes $50,000 a year; he/she simply cannot afford it.) So, assuming our buyer can afford what we are trying to sell, how do we actually sell it?

Now, let's press pause. You might be thinking that in your position, you don't have to be a sales person. *Everyone is a sales person.* We must constantly sell ourselves to our partners, bosses, customers and vendors. Sales is a basic skill that everyone needs but many people do not have.

Selling is really not about "hard" sales at all. In fact, I don't often make a hard close because that puts my clients on the defensive. Rather, I typically sell by educating the customer and creating a need within them for my product. Sales get easier if you understand what kind of person is across the table from you.

There are many different personality tests, but my favorite is the DISC personality test. It splits people into four different buckets, each of which should be approached differently, especially when it comes to sales. These four buckets are: D-Dominant, I-Influential, S-Steady and C-Conscientious. If you can quickly identify the personality type sitting across from you, you have an astronomically better chance of meeting your goal while wasting a lot less time.

DISC tests are available online, and they are extremely useful. It would greatly behoove you to take this test yourself because it will help you understand how you show up in the world and how to read others who are interacting with you. This will make you an immensely better salesperson, negotiator and human being.

Obviously, there's a lot to consider in these nine pillars of the New Curriculum, but I think you'd agree that each plays a significant role in positioning us for successful living. They've always been important—we should have been teaching these principles in our schools from the beginning—but in our changing world they are more critical than ever to living your dreams. I highly recommend revisiting this chapter again and again until each pillar of the New Curriculum becomes an integral part of your life.

Chapter 6: WHY PAYING YOUR DUES IS BULLSHIT

That's right: PAYING YOUR DUES IS BULLSHIT. Sorry if this offends, but I am a lot more sorry for the people who live their lives paying dues and never getting ahead.

Our equation DESIRE + PERSPIRE = SUCCESS is our cornerstone philosophy. The PERSPIRE part represents hard work. The hard work part is important, but it's only half of the equation.

Our society teaches us that you'll succeed if you work hard enough. If that were true, the vast majority of Americans would be rich. Millions of people work hard year after year and never grow wealthier. Why? Because they're missing the other part of the equation: DESIRE. When you're working for someone else's dream—someone else's DESIRE—your hard work isn't fueling your own success. It's fueling someone else's.

The idea of "paying your dues" comes out of this mentality—work long enough for someone else, and eventually it will magically evolve into working for yourself. Again, if that were true, pretty much every dues-payer would be rich. Paying dues doesn't get you ahead in society—it simply keeps you moving with the herd, with all the other schmucks who are paying *their* dues. To obtain a different result, you have to have an ANTI-HERD mentality. It is not enough to work hard; you also have to work *smart*. You have to go against the flow and start working toward your own DESIRE.

Author Tim Ferriss, author of one of my favorite books, *The 4-Hour Workweek*, warns against falling into the snare of W4W, meaning *work for work's sake*. W4W is an old-world, Second Wave paradigm because taken literally, that's *exactly* what paying dues is about— working for the sake of work. In our PERSPIRE/HARD WORK paradigm, we don't work for work's sake. We work for PURPOSE.

Remember in Chapter 2 when we talked about starting with **why**? We were talking about figuring out your own PURPOSE. ***Working for purpose*** means applying your hard work *toward your own purpose*, not someone else's. By today's standards, this is a non-conventional, anti-herd approach, but you won't meet the equation for success without it. You must PERSPIRE for your OWN DESIRE. When you understand what it truly means to *work for purpose*, you understand why paying your dues (i.e., working for someone else's dream) is BULLSHIT.

Please hear me on this. No one—NO ONE—gets ahead by paying their dues. They only get ahead when they *stop* paying dues and start working toward their own purpose. That's the myth debunked. Dues-paying only works when you STOP DOING IT.

Let's discuss this notion as it relates to the law firm model—again, the one with which I have the most experience. If you want to make partner at a law firm, you're going to have to work 10-12 years at a big firm, move up the ladder, and then *hopefully* be offered the opportunity. That's paying your dues, in my perspective. It is a long haul for a *maybe* chance, one day. The chance gets even smaller if you are a woman who dares to have a child and family life outside of the law firm. Women are punished for these choices. Either way, the odds are not in your favor. That's why I think paying your dues is bullshit.

My DESIRE+PERSPIRE=SUCCESS equation led me to start my own law firm at age 24. Want to make partner at a big law firm before you are thirty? Here's how you do it: *Start your own.* Bring in business to your own law firm and grow that firm to a seven-figure business. Then, watch as lawyers line up to buy your firm and find out how you did it.

Think this is too good to be true? It's not. It happens all the time. In fact, a few different law firms came to me through the years to offer me that very same opportunity (or something similar).

But here's the thing: I guarantee none of these law firms would have an interest in me if I were still "paying my dues" at some other firm. NONE. But now that I *work for my own purpose* and PERSPIRE toward my own DESIRE, my SUCCESS is apparent.

This is what I mean by an anti-herd mentality. When my friends told me, "I'm going to be a lawyer and I'm going to work for 15 years until I make partner," I laughed. Then I did exactly the opposite of what everyone else did. So far, it's served me pretty well.

My amazing mother always said, "If all your friends are jumping off the bridge, are you going to do it, too?" (I call my mom's advice *Nanaisms* because Nana is my Mom's name. Adorable, isn't it?)

I'm sure your parents have given you similar advice in your life. And yet, ironically, that when it comes to the decision of where to go to college and what to do with our life, our parents seem to forget that old adage and now effectively tell us to jump of the bridge with everyone else. "You have to be a doctor or a lawyer, you have to be an accountant, you have to take over the family business,"——those mandates come from the herd mentality that this-or-that career path is the one that leads to success. We are advised not to jump off the bridge with our friends when our parents believe it's the wrong choice, but yet they believe (like almost everyone else) that there is only one prescribed pathway to success that everyone should follow.

It's not entirely their fault. We've been effectively programmed this way for generations. But that mentality is completely false. In this day and age, more and more people are becoming extraordinarily successful by going 100% against the herd and against the grain—doing what everyone else didn't think to do because they were busy paying dues.

These successful people are chasing opportunities and building systems by combining 2 or 3 things that do not usually mesh, and they are building an amazing language around that new systems that they've built. Look at Elon Musk, look at Steve Jobs, look at Mark Zuckerberg, look at Bill Gates. These are the shapers of the new universe. When asked whether you will go with the herd, think about whether you want to be Elon Musk or John Doe.

Do you want to be herded like cattle? Or do you want to be one of those people who are shifting the planet?

If you want to be shifting the planet, which I believe you do, then every time you hear people are doing one thing—do the other thing. Believe me, the level of success in life you will lead as a result will be greater than your most insane fantasies. Spiritually, I believe that if something appeals to us, it's meant for us. The only separation between *wanting* it and *having* it is simply putting in the work.

What does this mean?

I refer once again to my equation for success. DESIRE + PERSPIRE = SUCCESS. You must get clear on your desire and then redefine the model. In that redefinition, having an anti-herd mentality, you'll find the riches of life.

Find that DESIRE, because it is what you're meant for. When you do, you will make all the money in the world by doing that thing and doing it well. Money is just an exchange of energy, so when you're putting into the world beauty and love and compassion and passion for what you were doing, money has to follow. It's a certainty. But you have to believe completely in who you are and what certainty understands—that all good things are coming to you.

This cannot be done by following the herd. If you are doing what everyone else is doing, you're not exceptional; you're ordinary. It's the hard truth, but if everyone can do it, what's the value?

Another of my favorite *Nanaisms* is "If it were easy, everyone would do it." What I'm saying here sounds simple, but *simple* and *easy* aren't the same thing. It's not easy to put your heart and face and life on the line to build your dream—it's scary as hell. If it weren't so scary, everyone would do it. But on the other hand, who wants to be working like an assembly line worker in a job that they hate for their entire life? You're at your job more than you're at home, so if you're contaminated with that negative energy day in and day out, who do you think you're going to be in your life outside?

There is no separation between work and life. *Your work is your life, and your life is your work.* That's why it's so important to *work for purpose*. When your work and your DESIRE don't mesh, how can you find happiness and fulfilment?

If you don't get this concept, it's time to wake up. We don't live in separate realities where we can stop what happened at work and pretend like our life is okay. Your work is necessarily your life. How are you going to live that life? How are you going to choose a job or career that day in and day out allows you to show up in the world in all areas the way you want to be seen—the way that is meant for you? Figure it out, because through life mapping as we discussed earlier, you'll actually figure out what it is that you want. At that point, it gets easier to go against the grain because your truth is going to be different from everyone else's. You can collaborate and share and understand what it is that drives others, because that's being compassionate; but to follow someone else's world just because they said that's the way to do it…

Are you going to jump off the bridge, too?

Paying dues is bullshit. Stop doing it. Work hard, but work toward your own desire.

Chapter 7: THE SOLUTION (An Introduction to IMPACT CIRCLES)

Now we come to my favorite part—where we take the NEW CURRICULUM that we discussed in Chapter 5 and integrate into a new way of thinking and doing. This is what I call THE SOLUTION.

How do we actually download this new education into our minds, making it accessible so we can live powerful lives and make lots of money while doing it? In the pages that follow, I'd like to present my own ideas of how I envision the Solution occurring. It won't necessarily come from any particular government, but rather from the private sector.

Primarily, I believe we must establish networks all around the country and the world to enable people of all different shapes, sizes and ages to come together. I believe these networks will be the new living communities where people eventually live in unison.

As an example of what I'm talking about, these communities might look a lot like the 55-plus communities that currently are popping up around the United States, where there are events and opportunities to meet people who live in that community. The primary difference would be the age restriction.

The thing about the 55-plus community is you have to be over 55 to be part of it. While this is mainly a good idea, it misses one important concept: There is no legacy building or teaching or mentoring that can happen in that setting. Think of what could be possible if that age barrier weren't in place, if the community were instead an integration of the young and the old coming together to learn the New Curriculum and implement it into their lives.

Under this new model of community, the young Millennial could benefit because it would give them access to the people who have built the businesses or who are the chairmans and CEOs of Fortune 500 Companies, and whom can actually get them in to the door of their dream job. Or, if the Millennial wants to be an entrepreneur, a seasoned business person can actually teach them about business building skills, sit on their advisory boards, etc. It would also benefit the older ones because it would give them a renewed sense of purpose and legacy in mentoring the younger generation.

So what, specifically, could we gain by establishing these networks? It would establish a free exchange of ideas in which people can come together and really speak about their strengths, as well as to educate, empower and inspire one another. It would also create an environment in which successful people can mentor the Millennial generation in a way that reduces their financial burden, in stark contrast to the student debt systems of higher education today.

If these communities existed, they could literally solve three major problems in our world:

1. The student debt epidemic (because people would have another option to success);
2. The recruiting problem (because companies and heads of industry could handpick the people best suited to work with them); and
3. The aging epidemic (because the older ones among us would find renewed purpose and a sense of legacy).

GUESS WHAT?!?!

These networks do exist!

The growing need for these types of communities recently led me to start IMPACT CIRCLES. In these networks, the bridge is built between seasoned professionals and students, thereby giving students access to opportunities without taking on tremendous debt. For the professionals, it gives us an opportunity to mentor students and recruit them into our organizations- WIN WIN WIN.

People are the lifeline of any organization. They are what make it run. This is why corporations spend millions of dollars to recruit and bring in the right people. What if the recruiting now happened organically through the networking that takes place within communities like this, both locally and around the world? What if the older, more experienced generation began to focus on the eleven **Guiding Principles** we mentioned in Chapter 1, and began teaching them to the Millennials in their community? It would allow the older generation, first of all to have impact; second, to build legacy; and third, never to spend a dime on recruiting again, because by the nature of their involvement with these young people, they would actually able to vet and place them within their organizations if they so choose! This presents an astronomical benefit as opposed to anything else that exists where you're truly disconnected from the people you are looking to bring into your organization.

Now, as these Impact Circles are growing all around the world and *en masse*, imagine the buying power that could result if this vision really took off. If every large organization had some people involved the community, every young person would have the potential and the ability to access that network and those corporations where otherwise they would not have such opportunity. In addition, the older generation would find a renewed sense of purpose beyond their children and their jobs.

Let's talk for a minute about the aging epidemic. Many of my clients in New York are spending between $15,000 and $25,000 a month for long term care, for example, in a nursing home, or with a home health care nurse or aide. Imagine how we could stop that particular epidemic from occurring because these older people would have a community who cares about them—people who see them as more than just an inheritance check that could be coming whenever they croak. Imagine the benefit of allowing them to build a different kind of legacy.

In all of my work with my clients, it really is amazing how little the money matters to them. With more money, we just do more sophisticated taxes, structuring and discounting and off shoring and whatever bullshit the other lawyers have invented to make it sexier to die with less of an impact financially. But what's the impact left on a person's life? If you're in that position, what's the legacy you leave for your children? What's the legacy you leave for the world? If this new paradigm were implemented, what would be your legacy then? You did something to help someone else, something you didn't have to do. You taught someone else something, and trust me, the payoff is more satisfying than anything money could buy. You would probably learn more and create more happiness in your life through giving this kind of work, through being part of this kind of community, than you ever could the way things are now.

The whole world shifts by tweaking the systems we have now in place just a little bit. I talk about establishing communities, but in reality the communities already exist. They now just need to be integrated, and the NEW CURRICULUM has to be brought to them, in order for true change to happen. We can no longer blame the government; the government can only do so much. We have to be the ones who buy into the idea, actually taking the steps forward as a society to move the needle. It is only with us that we must look for the treasure to build a better tomorrow for our children and for our grandchildren.

As I was walking along the Hawaiian beach as I wrote this chapter, I was feeling the waves crashing on my feet, just loving life. I looked to my left and I saw a man with headphones on and a metal detector looking for treasure. The ironic thing is that if he had just looked over his left shoulder, he would have seen the treasure all along: the Hawaiian sunrise. The beach meeting the water. The people in love with life and with each other. That's the treasure, but he was too busy looking externally for something he will never find.

If we go through life with headphones on, never looking at each other, how can we possibly see all the gifts that are right in front of our faces? How can we hear the messages that the Creator is sending us? How can we understand interaction with humans if we don't interact with humans? Technology is a wonderful thing; it has allowed for information to come to us easily. It has allowed for all these wonderful things to happen, but it's not a substitute for human interaction, because we are perfect in our own minds. If we didn't think something was perfect, why would we do it? It's in our human interactions that our challenges come to the forefront. So why don't we actually interact? What are we afraid of? How much longer do we have to live in a world where we have stopped loving each other?

It seems to me that the Solution is clear. We just have to start continue implementing Impact Circles around the world, where once again we start understanding life and actually living.

It's going to take all of us, though. To learn more about Impact Circles and find out how you can start one on your college campus or professional community, please reach out to us at www.msnatalienation.com and look for the impact circle dropdown.

Chapter 8: MILLENNIALS AS STAR EMPLOYEES

So many companies don't know what to do with Millennials. If you lead one of these companies, hopefully going through the Guiding Principles and integrating the New Curriculum will help you bridge the gap between you and your company and your Millennial workforce.

Employers must understand one essential characteristic of the Millennial Generation when it comes to work:

MILLENNIALS ARE PURPOSE DRIVEN.

They will only work and give you their time if they believe in what you're doing and if they feel appreciated for what they bring to it.

I hear people talk all the time about how Millennials act "entitled." Actually, it's not an entitlement at all. In fact, if older generations had one-tenth of the debt most Millennials are carrying, there is no doubt in my mind that there would have been a major uprising in the U.S. by now! How can we expect a generation of workers to take on $200,000-$300,000 dollars' worth of debt and be happy about it? Even worse, many in this generation find out that they didn't even *need* a college degree to get the job they have.

The difference between the Millennial worker and the worker of the previous generation is *access*. Years ago, a young person did not have access to contacts and opportunities without "paying their dues" and working up a company hierarchy. Today, that has all shifted as a result of the Internet and the ability to sell things online. Millennials have a level of access that enables them to be independent where the previous generations did not. If they are going to agree to give up their independence to work for your company, they must really *love* your company because you have amazing systems, amazing people, most importantly, PURPOSE.

Technology

Once again, let's go back to the law firm as an example. Many law firms still run the way they did in the 1970s. I know, because I have worked in them. I own one now (which is *not* the 1970s model). At one time, I had a partner, an 84-year-old gentleman who had all paper files and had no experience with technology.

That experience taught me that the only thing that works nowadays is to give a concrete structure to your employees and to have the right technology in place. I can tell you for certain that without these elements in place, Millennials in particular will stay away from your company in groups.

WHY? Because in 5 seconds or less, Millennial workers can sniff out the problems occurring in the company with the limitations placed upon them because of the company's technological shortfalls. As a result, they will want to make it better, and when they don't have access to the powers that be to implement that change, they will leave because they feel unheard and unappreciated. It's a shame, because honestly, they have ideas that probably would take your business to the next level. With Millennials, what's important is having regular team meetings where they feel heard and appreciated, taking their feedback into account and really understanding the technological steps you have to take so people can do less ground work and more *real* work.

Work Culture

The next thing Millennials consider in the work place is the culture of the company. Is it well defined? Do people understand that they are working as a team to infuse this culture into the company's vision and bring the right products to the market? If that culture is not defined and well established, you will not have a committed workforce. When the next person comes along who's willing to pay them a few extra dollars and perhaps give them health insurance, they will be out the door before you can blink.

Since nearly everyone has a degree today, the degree is no longer a differentiator for the Millennial employee. The differentiator is finding purpose driven people who can be passionate about your vision. For that to happen, though, they have to *understand* the vision and the culture of the company. Can you express your company vision? Is it posted everywhere for all your staff to see? If not, you are probably losing a staff member at this very moment.

In my first law firm job, I didn't understand what the levels of control were, or to whom I was accountable. I was told to read the big green book to learn about this subject matter. I was offered no training and was not told about the company's mission, vision or reason for being. Millennial workers are unlikely to stay in such a culture for long.

What owners need to understand is that without encouraging your staff and focusing them around a common goal and culture, you are wasting money and time on your recruitment efforts. Every new person coming into your company will leave within in a sixth-month period.

We have to do better than that. All the time, all the money, all the blood, sweat and tears that you are sacrificing to bring in clients can be lost because of the miscommunication (or no communication at all) happening between you and your client-facing workers. You must empower your employees around your vision and mission and ensure that your employees are fluent in the language that your company wants to articulate to the outside world. Without this, your foundation is at best, unsteady and at worst, one bad month away from bankrupting your company.

The way to change this dynamic is to create a company culture where people are committed to doing a great job, and *understanding what a great job means to you* based on very simple parameters. It's the only way that you can truly build a business that can be a mammoth. Otherwise, your resources are limited to your money and your time. When we limit anything to our time, especially, it's extremely limited because there are only 24 hours in a day. How much work can one possibly do? I bet you didn't start a business so that all you do is work 24 hours a day. I know I didn't. So perhaps it's time for us to reevaluate—to take a step back and really understand where our employees are, what role they would like in the company and where they would feel their strengths will be most utilized. Perhaps it's time for us to allow them to utilize their strengths, to take their interests into account to allow them to help us grow our companies. It would be a compete shift from how things are currently done, but the companies who embrace this concept will become mammoths in the next 15 years.

Everything is changing in the work force. Companies will no longer look the way they once did, and in fact many of them don't anymore. For the most part, all the best places to work in the world are tech companies that have embraced this methodology. Too many small business owners, and even some Fortune 500 companies, still don't understand these ideas. This absolutely has to change.

As I said at the beginning of this chapter, many companies don't know what to do with Millennials, so they don't really try. The problem with that thinking is that *Millennials are the future.* That means if you own a company and you want a legacy that continues beyond your death, you must embrace Millennial workers and create an environment in which they would want to work. Hopefully, by implementing the New Curriculum into your company's curriculum and building a strong culture, your business can thrive with the Millennial worker as the backbone of the company.

Chapter 9: MILLENNIALS AS BUSINESS OWNERS

So perhaps you're a Millennial, and you have decided that working at a company is not for you at all. You want to be in business for yourself. What should you do?

Number one: Don't take on debt if you can avoid it—and avoid it like the plague—because the debt will wear you down.

Number two: You don't necessarily need a regular college degree, or an advanced degree, in order to start your business. There are exceptions, of course; if you plan to be a lawyer or doctor, you'll have to go through those educational requirements. But for the moment, let's talk about businesses that aren't necessarily credentialed in that way, meaning by law there is no requirement that you have a certain degree.

If you start one of these businesses (also known as non-professional businesses), you can start it at any time, whether it's after college, after law school, after medical school, after your M.B.A., or at fifteen years old. The business that's going to be successful is going to be one that merges your passions. So, for example, if you love traveling and you also love writing and dancing, you might make a really great travel blogger who dances around the world. If it excites you, you can make money with it.

The Internet now allows us to live extremely mobile lives, due in large part due to selling platforms like Amazon and social media. In case you hadn't realized, you have the ability to live on your own channel, broadcasting to the world 24/7. That "channel" is your social media presence—Facebook, Twitter, Instagram, Snapchat, etc. Imagine now what advertising and marketing can be done on these sites. That level of marketing used to be unattainable because of the cost of television, newspaper, and traditional media advertisements. Today, by virtue of having a great social media presence and the right network and your passions aligned, YOU can start a multimillion dollar business, working the hours you want to work wherever in the world you want to be.

Do you understand how lucky we are to be alive at this time? We're in a position where we can actually live Tim Ferriss' reality as he describes in *The 4- Hour Workweek*. What magic could fill your life if all you had to do to sustain yourself was work four hours a week?

Make a list and figure it out. Go back to the chapters on living your dream and mapping your life if need be. Who are you beyond your work? If you really love your work and you're able to do it anywhere because you're living your passion, you'll never work a day in your life. You'll just make money doing what you love.

What do I love? I love bringing justice to people and protecting them and their families. I also love speaking and writing. What could be better than having the ability to speak on panels, write this book and speak about the protective nature of my legal business, as well as encourage young Millennials and older people to live the life they've always envisioned living?

If I can do that kind of thing every single day—if I can run groups and hold seminars and speak around the world based on that passion—that's not work. That's fun! That's my idea of my highest capacity of living. That is what I want to do for the rest of my life.

What do you want to do for the rest of your life? Think about it. What is the life you want to lead? Find the answer to that question and work backwards from there. Let's plan our ideal lives, then live them. What does that look like to you? To me, it's speaking around the world on the subject matter I just discussed, as well as having a beautiful family—being a committed and loving wife, having an adoring husband and two to three gorgeous children, while I also am building my dream career to be able to empower and inspire every single person I meet.

What's Your Dream?

Some questions that can help you answer this question include the following:

1.   What pulls at your heart strings?

2.   What would you do for free?

3.   What do you love so much that you do not care if you got paid for it?

The answer to those questions—that THING—is the thing that's going to get you paid. It's so ironic, isn't it? The things that we would do for free are actually what would make us the most money because they are natural tendencies playing on our natural strengths, doing work we love. We don't have to work so hard to do them well; we can just enjoy doing them, and that enjoyment and that passion and that purpose can touch the people that we inspire with our individual missions.

I know what you might be saying to yourself: *I'm scared! I want to be safe! I don't want to take risks!*

Friends, do you want to be safe, or do you want to live YOUR life? Do you want to continue making excuses, or do you want to live YOUR life? Do you want to kill yourself before you've even started living, or do you want to live YOUR life?

I can't answer those questions for you; I can only answer them myself. For me, I'm stepping in my purpose, and I'm owning everything that I need to live MY life. I have a law firm in New York City, and in that role I inspire and touch lives every single day. I'm *living*. Are you?

And lo and behold, we have arrived at the main purpose of this book. This book isn't really about some secret formula to change the world. All the things we've talked about lead to one purpose. This is just about you living your ***PURPOSE***. It's about you doing every day what you were born to do--waking up and saying, "My life is freaking amazing, how blessed am I, and it's so amazing that I want to spread the love to other people so that they can live amazing lives, too." When you do that thing you love every single day, when you wake up wanting to share the glory that is your life because you feel that this is the life you've always imagined and dreamed of and it surpasses every expectation you ever could have had, that's when you're in heaven. Do this, and you transform the world.

That's what life is all about, but we get in our own way and we make excuses and we make justifications. It's all bullshit. Stop making excuses for your life. Your life is your life. The most important thing in your life right now is the fact that you are living. Without life, without the breath that we need, how can we worry about anything else? Without breath, we are literally dead. So breathe in, and let the breath of what makes you feel alive completely invigorate your mind, body and soul, because that breath is what will now be breathed into each and every person whose life you touch on your individual mission.

LIVE YOUR DREAM! READY, SET, LIVE!

Epilogue

We've now come to the last chapter. I hope you have had as much fun reading this as I have had writing it. How blessed are we to be living life right now!

We have fallen in love with ourselves and understand that we are ever powerful to create the life we want. Just as I was thinking about how I should end this book, I met a beautiful mother on the beach. She told me about her friend, a military member who continued to serve in the military despite his blindness.

Despite his blindness.

This man did not let his blindness become an excuse for not serving in the military.

What are your excuses? Are you ready to part with them to start really living your dream? Have you defined that dream? Have you defined your own struggle so that you can begin to overcome it?

Have you finally realized that being extraordinary means going the exact opposite way of everyone else? If you have, you've gotten the message of this book.

Friends, you are loved. You are special, you are everything. Start acting like it.

Remember, through the lens of each other's eyes, we see the world.

I see you and I LOVE YOU.

NOW, GET TO WORK!

Made in the USA
Middletown, DE
12 July 2017